To: My Dear Pal
From: Your Friend
Cossie

Hope you enjoy some of mine
and Jackie's childhood Memories

God Bless you,
Jackie Bodden /09

Mr. Arthur's North Church Street

Joanne Sibley

Introduction to "A Cayman Childhood Remembered"

If you leave the bustling George Town waterfront with its tourists, taxis, and tour buses and head up on North Church Street you'll come to the three neat wooden buildings featured in the painting opposite. Look carefully for them because the artist has edited out some neighbouring modern concrete structures. She did that so the scene looks just like it must have done at the time the children in this volume of stories were growing up, and, as you read, you will recognize the home, the store, and the printing shop.

Anybody who knows Cayman at all well will also recognize the children who grow up in this book along with their parents, as well as many of the neighbours, friends, and assorted characters who fill its pages. If you don't, this introduction is not going to tell. As the saying goes, "That's for me to know and you to find out." And also because this delightful little collection of tales resides so comfortably in the land of storybook fiction.

The author first published the stories in three modest paperback volumes produced from 1981 to 2004. I don't think they claim to be great works of literary importance, but they lovingly and charmingly tell of times gone by. Still within living memory but how far away they seem. I have lived in Cayman just long enough to be able to relate to the way things used to be as described in the stories, and I fell in love with them. It was my idea to set all the stories into one hardbound volume as a more fitting repository for these little gems of Cayman history and culture.

The original of the painting hangs on the wall of The Cayman National Corporation board room and "Daddy," the hero of these stories (and one of my heroes too), unveiled it for us in the presence of "Mama" and some of the children you are going to read about.

Peter A. Tomkins, M.B.E.
George Town, July 15, 2007

Text Copyright 2007 by Jackie Bodden.

To protect the privacy of relatives and friends,
their names have been changed.

ISBN 0-9785936-4-2

STORY INDEX

ON THE ISLAND OF CAYMAN	1
BY THE SEASHORE OF CAYMAN	97
IN THE RAYS OF A CAYMAN SUNSET	195
GLOSSARY	287

ON THE ISLAND OF CAYMAN

By
Jackie Bodden

Cover By Susan Acree
Illustrated by Lisa Webb

CONTENTS

1.	ISLAND FAMILY	7
2.	THE SEVEN-MILE BEACH	11
3.	THE MYSTERY WOMAN AND THE SMUDGE POT	16
4.	TENDER CARE	20
5.	INSIDE THE PRINTING SHOP	25
6.	CAMPING	29
7.	EYEGLASSES FOR A CAYMAN WEDDING	33
8.	FROGS AND WATERLILIES	38
9.	THE CALM BEFORE THE STORM	43
10.	THE STORM	46
11.	THE BIG ALMOND TREE	52
12.	PIRATES AND DUPPIES FOR HALLOWEEN	57
13.	WASHERWOMAN'S SONGS	62
14.	THE SAND HILL	67
15.	DADDY'S CHRISTMAS LIST	72
16.	A FREE RIDE FOR OLD SMOKEY	77
17.	THE CASTLE	81
18.	NOT A YELLOWBIRD FALLS	85
19.	WHERE SEA BREEZES BLOW	90

*To Daddy and Mama
With Love*

1

ISLAND FAMILY

On an island forgotten by time where periwinkle flowers grew wild and coconut trees waved long branches in the breeze where white sand beaches, sprinkled with seashells, stretched for miles—there a little girl named Jackie laughed and played and sang.

Actually, she was not a little girl anymore. She liked to think that she was quite big for her ten years, even though she was the youngest of three sisters. Jane, the eldest sister, had green eyes and dark brown hair and spoke with a soft, gentle voice. Judy, the second sister, had blonde hair and eyes as blue as the Caribbean Sea that surrounded the island. Jackie, with her large green eyes and light-brown hair, dared to believe that she could outrun any girl her own age on the island. She played outdoors all year round and never tired of swimming in the cool sea water. She ran barefoot and felt as free as the yellowbirds that sang in the banana trees. She was a happy island girl.

Every morning Jackie sat in the kitchen with Daddy and Mama and watched the sun as it peeked through the swaying branches of the coconut trees. While Daddy and Mama drank their first cup of coffee, Jackie drank hot chocolate and listened to the birds as they chirped in the trees.

"Mother," Daddy said one morning, "I'll be in town a long time today. The boat is bringing a big order for the store." Jackie was happy because she liked all-day suckers and hardtack crackers, and she knew that Daddy had ordered them. Daddy looked over at Jackie, winked, and smiled. He knew what she was thinking. She liked to see Daddy smile. His blue eyes twinkled, and his gold tooth shined among the white ones. Jackie did not like to think of him having to lift heavy sacks of sugar and cases of canned food. Still, she knew that, despite his slim frame, Daddy was very strong.

"It's all right," Mama said in her gentle way. "I'll keep dinner warm until you get here." Mama was pretty and jolly. Jackie liked to hear her laugh. Her laughter was contagious; everyone around her laughed too.

Daddy finished his cup of coffee, took his handkerchief from his pocket, wiped his mouth, and went to open the store. He walked across the street, fitted the key into the lock, and the door swung open. It was 7:00 a.m.

Jackie was thinking how lucky she was that they had such a good store. Daddy's father, Papa, had built it long ago when Daddy was a boy. He built it of island ironwood because he wanted it to last a long time. Although many storms had tried, they had never been able to shake it.

Mama poured another cup of coffee and smiled as she looked toward her bougainvillea plant. She loved flowers and probably was glad that she had moved that plant from the front yard to the back. It had not blossomed well in the front yard because the salt air had stunted its growth. But now the bougainvillea plant was blooming. In the back yard, outside the kitchen window, it proudly displayed its beautiful pink blossoms and was as much a part of the island as the banana trees just beyond it.

Mama drank her second cup of coffee and then went to see if baby brother was awake. John was the newest member of the family, and he would soon be two years old.

Jackie went to the front porch and sat in the swing. As she looked toward the sea, she wondered what it would be like to live in a faraway land. For sure, she thought, it would not be better than Cayman. A butterfly perched on the swing, and its yellow-and-black wings fluttered as the swing moved back and forth. It was the prettiest butterfly Jackie had ever seen.

Suddenly, Baw Baw came through the gate. As she hurried toward the kitchen, her full skirt fluttered behind her. For many years, she had cooked for Daddy and Mama, and she was almost a part of the family. She was jolly and her little black eyes danced when she laughed. Soon a hearty breakfast would be ready.

Jackie watched as the clerk began her day in the grocery store. It was 8:00 a.m. Daddy left the store and walked toward the printing shop. He had been a printer for years. His printing shop was built across the yard, only a short distance from the house. Suddenly Jackie heard a familiar noise and knew that it was the printing press rolling.

She was thinking of Baw Baw's tasty cooking when she heard "Breakfast is ready." No one needed to be called twice.

Daddy asked the blessing as he sat at the head of the table. "For what we're about to receive, O Lord, make us humbly thankful." He said the same blessing at every meal. Jackie knew that Papa had said that blessing also.

Jackie ate slowly as the delicious corn porridge slid down her throat. Baw Baw had cooked it with coconut milk, and she liked the taste of coconut. The table rocked slightly as they ate. Perhaps one of her sisters was wiggling her knees beneath the yellow-and-white-checked tablecloth.

"I bought some fish this morning that Jim caught," said Mama. "We'll have that for dinner."

John wiggled in his highchair and clapped his tiny hands as Daddy sang his son's favourite song.

Two little fishes in a brook
Jim Jim caught them with a hook
Baw Baw fried them in a pan
John John ate them like a man.

2

THE SEVEN MILE BEACH

School vacation had begun and giggles were heard everywhere as children played and sang and swam.

"This afternoon we'll go swimming," Daddy said with a twinkle in his eye. His three girls shouted with glee. Swimming was their favourite sport.

As Jackie helped Mama make the beds and sweep the hardwood floor, she thought of the clear water and white sand beaches. She wished she could move the hands on the clock forward, because they moved too slowly.

Finally it was noon, and Baw Baw called them to dinner. Jackie's eyes scanned the table, and she realized that Baw Baw had cooked her favourite dinner. She saw turtle meat and rice, baked bananas, cassava, and coconut cream pie. She piled large servings on her plate and picked up her fork, only to find that she was no longer hungry. Her fork moved in circles on her plate as she nibbled on a bite or two. She was too excited to eat dinner.

After dinner, Daddy said, "All right girls, I'll take a short nap. During that time, you may shake the mango tree and gather mangoes to eat in the sea."

Jane, Judy, and Jackie clapped their hands. They liked eating juicy, sweet mangoes while playing in the water.

Judy climbed the tree and shook it gently, and the ripe fruit tumbled down. Jane was picking up the mangoes and putting them in a heap, but Jackie picked up only one golden mango and ran toward a tree stump. As she sat on the tree stump she realized she was hungry. Her sisters threatened to tell Daddy that she did not help them, but she could think only of the mango. As she bit into the luscious fruit, the juice trickled down her arms and dripped off her elbows.

Jane and Judy picked up the mangoes and walked toward home, but Jackie sat on the tree stump and continued eating the mango until the seed was bare and white. Then she went home, the streaks of golden mango juice still on her arms.

Daddy called to say that he was ready to go swimming. Mama would stay at home with baby John, as the sun would be too hot for him at the beach. The three girls, in bathing suits, with arms full of mangoes, ran to meet him. Today was special. Usually they went swimming in the sea across the street from their house. There the water was crystal clear and calm, but the sharp rocks hurt their feet. Today, they were going to swim at the Seven-Mile Beach.

"Why is it called the Seven-Mile Beach, Daddy?" Jackie asked. "And why is Cayman known as the island that time forgot?"

"Seven-Mile Beach lets people know how long that lovely stretch of beach is, little Dupso," said Daddy. "It is supposed to be one of the most beautiful beaches in the world. And Cayman is called the island that time forgot because people around the world do not know of its beauty yet. Someday this peaceful little island will be crowded with visitors, all of them coming to swim on the Seven-Mile Beach."

Jackie could not imagine what crowded beaches would look like. And anyway, she liked the island just the way it was. She also liked when Daddy called her "little Dupso", because that was his special name for her.

"We're here," someone shouted. They had arrived at the place called Two Pines. High against the blue sky the majestic pine trees stood adding their touch of beauty to the beach.

The girls raced toward the water. Mangoes fell as they ran. The ones that didn't fall on the beach were thrown into the water. The girls were diving at once, picking up the mangoes from the white sand beneath the water. It was fun, and now Jackie ate the delicious mangoes while the water washed the juice from her elbows.

Jackie was remembering the time that she learned to swim. Daddy had brought her here. She was little then, and Daddy told her to hold onto his shoulders, and he would swim with her on his back. When he had swum farther out than she could stand, he put his head under the water and began to dive. He slipped Jackie's hands from their grasp on his shoulders as he dived deeper. She was still on the surface of the water and her feet and hands kicked and splashed. She was learning to swim. But beneath the water, Daddy's watchful eye followed her every move. By the time he came to the surface, his youngest girl could swim.

Jackie was a good swimmer now, and she liked the salty taste of the sea. With graceful movements resembling a mermaid, she moved through the water as her eyes followed the white sand beaches, pine trees, and blue sky. Here and there a few families were scattered along the beach. She saw a thatch hut in the distance. It had been built as a shelter from the sun for people who collected seashells.

The three girls had another idea: they wanted to gather seashells. They ran along the beach, each sister in a different direction. They then stooped and moved slowly as their eyes scanned for seashells.

Jackie picked up a delicate pink-and-white sunbeam shell that looked like a butterfly. She admired it, and then she carefully put it in her shell-bag. Sprinkled here and there were brown-and-white shells shaped like fans and yellow sunbeam shells. Soon she spotted a beautiful queen conch shell and wanted to take it home. Unfortunately, it was too big to carry, so she moved on. The shell-bag became heavy with colourful seashells, and finally she had enough. She would go back to Daddy.

As she tried to find her way back, she realized she had been so busy gathering seashells that she had not noticed she was far away from her family. She sat down and cried. Did they go home and leave her? Would she be able to find her way back home? Suddenly someone asked "What's the matter?" Jackie looked up at the faces of her sisters. She hugged one and then the other.

Daddy called and said it was time to go home. On the way home, Jackie thought about this happy day at the beach and of a sweet Mama waiting at home with baby brother. She remembered how happy she had been to see her sisters when she was lost and a poem came to mind that she had learned in school a few weeks earlier. Its words comforted her.

> *There is no friend like a sister*
> *In calm or stormy weather,*
> *To help one on the tedious way*
> *To fetch one if one goes astray,*
> *To lift one if one totters down,*
> *To strengthen whilst one stands,*

3

THE MYSTERY WOMAN AND THE SMUDGE POT

The next day, as Jackie and Judy traded seashells, Sally came around the corner of the house. She was swinging a smudge pot in her hand. The smudge pot smoked furiously, and although the smoke was supposed to keep the mosquitoes away, many followed her. Sally was an old lady on the island. Even though she was loved, no one claimed her. It seemed she had no family.

Both girls became quiet and listened to what Sally said as she talked to herself. "Inny warship inny be here tomorrow. Inny me dress up." No one knew what "inny" meant, but she said it often. She did not speak proper English, but everyone understood her.

Her hair was gray and her skin was dark, and she had not been to school because she had a difficult time learning. She went to houses, knocked on kitchen doors, and always said, "Me here." She was announcing her arrival for either breakfast, dinner, or supper.

"Sally I'll give you your dinner in a minute," said Mama, as she looked out the door.

Immediately Sally started telling Mama all the news. "Inny warship inny be here tomorrow, inny me dress up." For someone who understood so little, Sally always seemed to remember the news. People often smiled and called her a walking radio, because she liked to spread the news.

She ate the tasty dinner that Mama gave her and said, "Want me pick up leaves? Want me work?"

"Yes, Sally," Mama said, "go across the street to the store and ask the clerk to send me some spaghetti." That must have been a hard word for her to remember, because as the girls continued to exchange seashells, they heard Sally say, "Spaghetti, spaghetti, spaghetti," but just as she stepped up in the door of the store, she stubbed her toe. "Oh, me forget it," she said. Then her eyes lit up and she smiled as she turned to the clerk and said, "Yes, me want some forget-it." The clerk reached over the counter and handed her the spaghetti. A happy Sally crossed the street.

She still jabbered on and on to Mama about the new dress that she wanted. Mama looked at Sally's old dress, her old torn stockings, and those dirty tennis shoes that she always wore on the wrong feet, and she felt sorry for her.

"Sally, you'll be pretty tomorrow," Mama said.

Jackie did not know what Mama had in mind as she said that, but she soon found out. She heard Mama's sewing machine buzzing. Before sunset, Mama had finished a new dress for Sally. She had talked to her friends and each one was working to make Sally look nice for the warship.

A neighbour bought new shoes for Sally; another lady

gave stockings, and yet another gave a pink bow for her hair. Mama got perfume and powder out of the store for her. Everyone was excited.

The next morning, Sally came out as usual, her smudge pot swinging in her hand, the mosquitoes still following her. She was happy with the gifts, but she wanted to put the new dress on over the old one. Finally a neighbour convinced Sally that she would have to take a bath if she wanted the new dress.

Before long, Sally was dressed in the colourful new dress with the pink bow in her hair, and Mama put her new shoes on the correct feet. Wearing dark red lipstick and face powder, she began her long walk to town to be sure that she was early for the warship.

Jackie, Judy, and Jane went inside the house to get dressed to go to town. Mama was wearing a pale-blue silk dress, and John was dressed in a little sailor suit. He was such a happy baby.

"Ship ahoy, ship ahoy!" the people shouted, as the warship came into view.

The island belonged to Britain, and everywhere British flags waved proudly in the wind. The mighty warship came from England and the friendly island people were letting them know that they were welcome.

When Jackie arrived in town, she saw crowds of people. Sailors were landing from small boats that had been launched from the warship. The Commissioner of the island stood at attention to welcome them, and a twenty-one-gun salute sounded through the town.

A parade moved through the center of town, and the band played the National Anthem while the people reverently sang,

*"God save our gracious King
Long live our noble King,
God save the King.
Send him victorious,
Happy and Glorious,
Long to reign over us,
God save the King."*

In the middle of the street, while the National Anthem was being sung, Sally danced. She did not know that it was considered improper to dance to that music. The pink bow hung lopsided in her hair, and she had forgotten to wear garters to hold up her stockings, so they fell to her ankles. She must have thought her new shoes were uncomfortable, because she had taken them off and put the left shoe on the right foot and the right shoe on the left foot. But she kept on dancing.

Jackie nudged Mama and they both smiled as they heard Sally say, "Inny me no care, Inny me Queen for a day."

4

TENDER CARE

The warship stayed for two days, and the celebrations continued day and night. But on the third morning when they awoke, the ship was nowhere in sight. It had moved on to another island.

"I want you to get the house in order so that we can begin painting tomorrow," Daddy said to Mama. "I'm in a hurry to get the painting done before the hurricane season begins."

"Yes, I know you're right," agreed Mama. "We do need to get that done before the storms hit."

The other children were asleep, but Jackie sat by the kitchen door listening. She was excited. Painting would be fun. She knew that each time the house was painted, they slept in the printing shop. The last time the house was painted, Jackie was quite small. She could not remember the fun of camping in the printing shop. But she had heard her sisters speak of it.

Daddy and Mama were discussing the colours they would paint each room, when suddenly Old Smokey, the stray cat, made a strange sound. They looked outside just as he displayed his catch. In his mouth he held a little mouse that he had caught in the woods. He dropped it on the ground and strutted back and forth.

"Good boy, Smokey, you're a good boy." said Daddy.

That seemed to be what Old Smokey was waiting for because he quickly ate his breakfast. Mama liked Old Smokey. She said she need never worry about mice getting into the yard as long as he was around.

As Daddy poured another cup of coffee, he mentioned that he would need Jane and Judy to work in the store. He knew that it would be a busy day, and the clerk would need them to help her.

Mama looked at Jackie and smiled as she said, "That will be all right. Jackie is a big girl now, and she can help watch the baby while I finish sewing the girls' new pajamas."

Jackie was happy that Mama trusted her to take care of baby brother John, but what she really wanted was to be old enough to work in the store. She wanted to weigh sugar and flour and cheese for customers. However, she would try to be a good girl and help Mama.

After breakfast, Mama began sewing. She had made two pairs of cool summer pajamas for her girls, so she needed only to make one more. Jackie picked up a big ball and took it to the back yard. Then she came back inside the house for little brother. As he smiled and clapped his hands, she remembered what Mama had told her.

"Children are like plants," Mama once said. "They need tender care to help them grow strong and healthy."

Mama had taught her long ago that love lightens labour, and she loved little brother, so today would be fun even if she could not work at the store. They played with the ball, and they played in the sandyard. Like most island yards, their yard was covered with sand. They lived too close to the sea to grow grass, but sand was pretty and it felt good under bare feet.

When it was noon, they went inside to eat dinner. Mama was still sewing, her foot moving back and forth on the pedal of the sewing machine. She looked tired, but she never complained. Sewing was not Mama's favourite work, and Jackie thought she heard her sigh.

Dinner was delicious, Baw Baw had cooked red beans with corned beef and dumplings. There was rice and golden cornbread to eat with it, and a glass of fresh lemonade was beside each plate. Mama said the lemonade helped to keep her children healthy. They drank it often.

"I'm proud of you," Daddy said as he looked across the table at Mama. "Our girls will be happy when they wear their new pajamas."

"Today's sewing is almost finished," Mama replied with a smile. She was happy that Daddy was proud of her.

As Mama sat down to finish sewing the pajamas, Jackie heard her say, "It's so sweet to labour for the ones we love, it's no wonder that maidens wed."

That night each girl took a cold bath in the big iron tub

with its funny legs. Daddy had bought it for his mother long ago with his first paycheck. Then each sister tried on her new pajamas. They were lovely. They were made of a soft material with lace stitching around the neck. In front was a bow. Jane's bow was pink. Her pretty dark hair looked nice with pink. Judy's bow was the same colour blue as her eyes, and Jackie's green bow matched her eyes.

They were happy as they climbed into their little beds. Mama always said that the nicest luxury a child could know was clean sheets and new pajamas. But Jackie was too excited to sleep. She knew that tomorrow night she would be camping in the printing shop, and she had been waiting a long time to see inside of it.

As she tried to sleep, she heard a mama bird calling her babies to their nest. Frogs croaked outside, and crickets chirped. A tiny light stole across the floor. Jackie got out of bed and tiptoed toward it as the hardwood floor creaked beneath her feet. Finally, she stood beside the light and realized it was a moonbeam. She bent forward and placed her open hand on the floor as she picked it up.

With the moonbeam dancing in her hand, she moved toward the window, and pretended to throw it outside, but it moved faster than her eyes. By the time she looked back at the floor, the ray of moonlight was already there. Quietly she crossed the room and crawled back into bed.

From her little bed just under the screened window, she saw the breadfruit tree blowing in the wind. It gave her a feeling of peace and calmness. Finally, she fell asleep with the sound of the waves splashing against the rocks. There was never a sweeter sound than the sound of the water gently moving against the shore. Jackie liked to think of it as God's lullaby through which He lovingly soothed a tired world to sleep.

5

INSIDE THE PRINTING SHOP

It seemed no time at all until it was morning. After breakfast, Daddy took Jackie by the hand and said, "Okay, little Dupso, I want to show you inside the printing shop. There are machines inside the printing shop that little girls are not allowed to touch, and Daddy wants to be sure that you are aware of it."

As they stepped inside the back door, Jackie noticed first the white walls and gray floor. It was bigger inside than she had imagined. Just inside the door, she saw a sink with splotches of black ink on it.

Daddy started his tour in the left-hand corner and moved down that wall. A counter had been built along the wall. Jackie saw a stack of envelopes on it with a paperweight on top. She picked up the paperweight and wished she could have it. The bottom of the paperweight was a solid piece of wood, shaped like a branch, and three monkeys sat on it. The first monkey held his hands over his ears. The second monkey held his hands over his mouth, and the third monkey held his hands over his eyes. Jackie read aloud the words that were written on the paperweight, "Hear no evil, speak no evil, see no evil."

As they moved along the counter, Jackie noticed a machine. Daddy explained that it was a hand-press machine, and that he used it to print government forms and addresses on envelopes. He showed her alphabets of all sizes and shapes. Then he began fitting some letters into a steel plate to form words.

"This is called setting up type," he said, "and the interesting thing about setting up type is that I must write the words backwards. After I finish, I hold a mirror in front of the type and read the words in the mirror to see if I've written them correctly."

"Do you make many mistakes?" Jackie asked.

"Yes, I do," Daddy laughed. "It's never easy to write words backwards." His fingers moved swiftly as he completed the words he was writing.

"Now would you like to read what I've written?" he asked. Jackie looked at the strange writing.

"It's my name," she shouted. "You wrote my name."

"Yes, I did," Daddy continued, as he held the mirror in front of the steel plate, while Jackie read aloud, "Jackie Bodden, George Town, Grand Cayman."

Daddy then put the steel plate into one side of the press and a sheet of paper in the other side. As he pressed the handle, an inked roller moved over the letters, leaving them ready for printing. Then the steel plate and the sheet of paper moved together, and Jackie's name and address appeared on the paper. The machine printed a sheet each second or two. Daddy printed hundreds each day on this machine.

As they moved further down the counter, Jackie saw neatly stacked packages under the counter.

"Daddy, do you have any surprises in those packages?" she asked.

Daddy smiled. "No, it's only paper - white paper, pink paper, yellow paper, and blue paper - and many envelopes," he said.

In the far front corner, Jackie saw Daddy's most comfortable chair. He sat in it when he was tired. With an open window beside it, he could view the house and grocery store with a glance. Sometimes Daddy sat in that chair by the window and smoked his pipe, and sometimes he took a nap. Jackie had seen that through the window when she had played outside.

They walked past the front door to Daddy's desk and chair in the right-hand corner of the printing shop. A big black typewriter was on the desk. Just above it, Daddy had hung a picture of a sailboat. Jackie's eyes scanned every detail of that sailboat with its sails blowing in the wind. Tiny waves rippled against the side of the boat, and the tip of each wave was white with foam. It reminded her of the many times that she had seen sailboats gliding through the sea. She wanted to look at the picture longer, but Daddy moved on.

In the right-hand corner at the back of the printing shop was the paper cutter. Daddy warned that Jackie must never touch this. It could cut off a little girl's fingers or even an arm in a second, he explained, and then he showed her how it worked. He took a piece of thick cardboard from under the counter. He placed it on the paper cutter and brought the sharp blade down with a bang. Jackie blinked her eyes and moved back. It scared her. Suddenly, she saw where the piece of cardboard had been. Two pieces had replaced the one.

"It cuts as clean as a whistle," Daddy said. "So do not ever go near it."

"I'll never touch it," Jackie promised. Daddy knew that he could depend on her. Then he took her by the hand, and they walked out the front door. Above the door and across the front of the printing shop, Jackie saw a sign. In big bold letters was written the word PRINTER.

6

CAMPING

Daddy began painting the living room, while Mama and the girls took clothes from the house and put them in the printing shop. They took pillows and quilts and stacked them on the counter and Mama mopped the floor. When she finished it was shining clean.

As soon as the chores were done, the girls ran to the back yard to play. They took John with them to the hammock that was tied under the naseberry tree.

Every island family had at least one hammock, made from a wide piece of canvas and stretching about eight feet long, with rope tied to each end. It was fun swinging in a hammock, but the girls knew they must never swing too hard. The rope could break and the person in the hammock could get hurt, so they remembered to be careful.

Baw Baw was cooking dinner as usual, since the kitchen did not need painting. Jackie went to the kitchen door and asked if she might please come inside. Baw Baw was busy, but she said, "I s'pose so."

Jackie would try not to get in the way. She sat in a

chair by the door for a while and just watched. Inside the kitchen, the walls and floor were light gray. A big iron stove was in one corner. It burned wood and had a long black stovepipe that went up through a hole in the top of the wall and took the smoke outside. It was on this stove that Baw Baw was cooking.

Jackie saw a huge pot of water boiling on the iron stove. Two lobsters crawled and wiggled on the table. They had been caught that morning and were still alive. Baw Baw picked one up, put it in the pot, and covered it with a lid. They heard a scratching sound inside the pot for a few seconds, as the lobster tried to crawl out. After a few minutes, Baw Baw took that lobster out and put the other one in. Then she took that one out also.

"May I help?" asked Jackie.

"I s'pose so; I sure could use some help today," replied Baw Baw.

So while Baw Baw kneaded and shaped bread, Jackie worked on the lobsters. She took a knife and hit the lobster's legs at the joints. Then as she pulled on the joints, the lobster meat separated from the shell. She put the meat in a bowl and the shell in a stack to be thrown away.

She was not allowed to eat lobster, even though she liked it. She had eaten it a couple of times, but it had made her feel sick. Red spots had appeared all over her, and Mama said that she was allergic to it. However, she liked helping Baw Baw get it ready for the others to eat. Helping made her feel important. But suddenly her right thumb felt strange and became swollen. It looked twice as big as her left thumb.

"I never saw the like of it," Baw Baw said as she

looked at it and shook her head. Then they saw a tiny cut by the fingernail. A piece of the lobster shell had pierced the skin, and because Jackie was allergic to lobster, her thumb was swelling. Baw Baw thanked her for helping and finished shelling the lobsters. She took out her biggest frying pan and put it on the stove. She put oil in it and onion and bell pepper. Then she stirred them around and put in the lobster and left it to cook slowly on the back of the stove.

Baw Baw opened the lid on the top of the stove and put in two more pieces of wood, because the oven needed to be hot before she could put the bread in it. After a while she walked to the side of the stove and opened the oven door. Since it was hot enough, she put the bread in.

Jackie became restless and went back out to play. She showed her sisters her fat thumb and how it tended to fall back down when she held it up.

The girls ran happily to the dining table that had been placed under a tree in the back yard. Baw Baw had planned a surprise for Jackie because she had been a good helper. As the others ate the delicious lobster, Jackie ate fried goggle-eyed fish. *It was probably the best fish in the world,* she thought. She also had fried green bananas and fresh baked bread.

That evening the three sisters went across the street to swim in the sea behind the store. They took turns pushing each other into the water. It was cool and refreshing. They played on a big rock in the shallow part of the bay. Occasionally, an old crab crawled out from under the rock. Judy was afraid of the crab, but Jackie and Jane poked sticks at it until it went back under the huge rock.

Suddenly, they saw a piece of pigiron that they often

played with. Since it was about the size of a grapefruit, they could lift it only when they were under the water. Whenever they brought the pigiron out of the water they had to roll it on the ground because it was very heavy. They often picked it up and walked beneath the water, because it held them down.

They said "eenie, meenie, minie, moe" to decide who would get to go first. Judy won. She dove down to the bottom and picked up the pigiron. Jackie and Jane watched as she walked a long way under the water with it. But soon she needed to breathe, so she dropped it and came to the surface. She was crying. She held up her hand to discover that one fingernail was missing. The pigiron had dropped on a rock instead of sand, and her finger was caught between it and the rock.

The three girls were crying as they showed the finger to Mama. She said that the iodine in the sea water would help to heal it.

That night each girl made herself a bed on the floor of the printing shop. They told stories and giggled. Daddy asked to see the fat thumb and sore finger and sang a song to suit the occasion.

I'm just a wounded soldier, returning from the war,
With a cut across my forehead and a half a dozen more,
My eyes are dim, I cannot see, and my head is hanging low,
I've got one shoe on the wrong foot, and I lost one big toe.

7

EYEGLASSES FOR A CAYMAN WEDDING

Aunt Bebe moved from crepe myrtle trees to oleander trees and then on to the hibiscus trees, cutting flowers as she went along. Jackie watched as the yard next door was stripped of its beautiful flowers. Aunt Bebe picked up a handful from beneath the avocado pear tree where she had stacked them and began taping them to the trunk and overhanging branch of the tree. What is she doing? Jackie wondered.

She jumped the fence and ran and stood beneath the tree. "May I please help?" she asked.

"Of course," Aunt Bebe answered. "First, hand me a bunch of pink oleanders." When Aunt Bebe had taped them to the tree, she continued, "Now a yellow hibiscus. Let's add purple crepe myrtles and next the pink oleanders again so that they form a pattern."

"You sure are making that old pear tree pretty," Jackie said. "How many more are you planning to put on it?"

"All of them. I know you are dying to know what is going on, you little inquisitive girl, so I might as well tell you," Aunt Bebe said with a chuckle. "There's going to be a wedding here this evening, so I'm decorating the yard."

"Oh," Jackie whispered. "May I come? Who is getting married?"

"Lydia and Aaron. She didn't seem concerned about the decorations, but she insisted that I borrow a pair of gold-rimmed eyeglasses for her to wear at her wedding. Says she'll not get married without them."

"That's strange," Jackie said. Aunt Bebe just laughed.

Flower after flower was taped not only on the trunk of the pear tree but also on a branch that hung down almost to the ground. When finally it was finished, Jackie thought that her arms were about to fall off.

"We'll take a break now," Aunt Bebe said, so Jackie went and stood outside the kitchen where Aunt Becky sat in the doorway.

Jackie saw out loud the beautiful archway of flowers for Aunt Becky. "I wish you could see them," Jackie told her. "When the wedding is over this evening I will read the Bible to you and also a chapter from *Ben Hur.*"

"I'll look forward to that," Aunt Becky said. Her big brown eyes had been blinded by cataracts before Jackie was born.

"Bebe, come here quick," Aunt Becky yelled, and Aunt Bebe came running. "Stand exactly where Jackie is standing. I just caught a glimpse of her face for the first time. Saw her big green eyes and her little round smiling face and the unruly bangs on her forehead."

Aunt Bebe did as her mother told her, but the moment had passed and Aunt Becky was once again blind. She reached out and hugged Jackie and said, "Praise be to

God. I saw your face."

In Aunt Bebe's hand was a pair of gold-rimmed glasses. She turned to Jackie and asked if she would go and tell Lydia to get her bath because the wedding would begin in two hours.

Jackie ran down the dirt path until she came to Lydia's house. She found her sitting on the sand beneath a breadfruit tree with a plate of fish stew in her lap. In her hand was a big fat flour dumpling that she rolled around and around in the coconut gravy before biting it. A radio beside her played love songs, and Jackie thought that fish stew had never smelled so good. She gave her the message from Aunt Bebe, but she seemed not to be listening.

The radio began playing *Tell me you love me just one more time,* and Lydia reached out and turned it off. "I want to save that song for my precious Aaron to listen to tonight, because it's his favourite song." Then she turned to Jackie and asked her to tell Aunt Bebe that she would see her shortly because she had taken her bath that morning.

Jackie had barely made it back to tell Aunt Bebe what she said when Lydia appeared at the kitchen door all out of breath, her white satin wedding dress over her arm. She stepped inside the door and disappeared in the house to get ready for her wedding.

When next Jackie saw her, she looked charming, her beaming face adorned with rouge and lipstick, a spray of forget-me-nots in her hair. Aunt Bebe slipped the gold-rimmed glasses on her and held up a mirror.

"These glasses make the whole outfit," Lydia said smiling. "And I can see so good with them. Just like they were made for me." Aunt Bebe just smiled.

The preacher arrived. Aunt Bebe was wearing a skirt of many colours that unfolded in hundreds of tiny pleats as she walked.

The time had arrived for the wedding, but the groom was nowhere in sight. Lydia sat in a chair outside, fanning with a thatch fan. Finally Aaron rounded the corner of the house with his black jacket over his arm. "I'm sorry I'm late," he said, kneeling beside his bride-to-be. He slipped on his coat and the wedding was about to begin.

Aunt Bebe held a tiny straw basket in her hand filled with purple and white periwinkle petals. "These are for your flower girl," she said.

"Flower girl? flower girl?" Lydia stammered. "I don't have no flower girl."

Aunt Bebe turned to Jackie. "How about you?"

"I can't," Jackie told her. "I'm not dressed for a wedding, and I'm barefoot." Jackie was remembering the time that she stood flower girl for her cousin. Mama had made a lovely dress with lace and ribbon and had a hair band of flowers in her hair. She remembered the organ playing and the church full of people, and *no, she was not dressed for a wedding!* Aunt Bebe woke her from her daydream. She was tying a garland of flowers around her ankle.

"Look at you," Aunt Bebe said. "As pretty a flower girl as I've ever seen in your little pink-and-white dress with your pink periwinkle flowers around your ankle." Aunt Bebe slipped the basket of petals in her hand and Jackie walked down the aisle beneath the pear tree, sprinkling periwinkle petals for the bride to crush beneath her feet.

Aunt Bebe stepped forward next, a red hibiscus in

her hair, her pleated skirt swaying. Then came the bride with a smile on her face and the gold-rimmed eyeglasses shining in the sunlight.

It was all so very pretty. The flowers on the pear tree blew in the breeze and finally the preacher said, "You may kiss the bride." As Aaron bent forward and kissed her, the eyeglasses fell to the ground. Jackie bent down and picked them up, but they felt light, and she realized that they had no glass in them. She bent down again and began searching the nearby sand, but Aunt Bebe touched her on the shoulder and whispered "It's okay. There was never any glass in them."

8

FROGS AND WATERLILIES

The freshly painted house looked new. Little handprints had disappeared beneath the recent coat of paint, and Mama smiled as she walked from the blue bedroom to the white living room and then to the pink bedroom.

Jackie liked the pretty house, but she was remembering the fun they had while camping in the printing shop. She was thankful that everything turned out well. Judy's finger was healing and a tiny new fingernail had begun to grow. Jackie's thumb was back to its usual size, and she vowed never to touch a lobster again.

All day long Mama and the girls mopped floors and put the house back in order. That night they were all tired.

"Let's spend the day at Grandma's house tomorrow," said Mama. Her girls answered with "Yes, yes, yes!"

Jackie got up early the next morning when the big

red rooster crowed outside her window. She thought it was his way of welcoming a new day.

After breakfast, they started their journey to Grandma's house. She lived several miles away at the part of the island called Spotts. Since they had no telephone, they were unable to let Grandma know that they were coming. However, when the car pulled up in her yard, she came to the door and shaded her eyes with her hands. Her face lit up with a big smile as she came out to the car and hugged Mama and Daddy and then the grandchildren, letting them know they were special to her.

"I'm so glad you could come," she said over and over. She was Mama's mother, and it was in this house that Mama was born.

Aunt Tes came around the corner of the house and greeted each one. Sweet, gentle Aunt Tes was special to them. She hugged Jackie and said, "How is Teenie Tiny?" That had been her name for each of Mama's children as they came along. And even though Jackie was quite a big girl now, and John was the baby, she still called Jackie "Teenie Tiny" out of habit.

As they walked inside the house, the soft lace curtains moved in the breeze. Even on the hottest days, a soft breeze blew at Spotts. Jackie always thought that it was the coolest part of the island.

While the grown-ups talked, Jackie went outside to look around the yard. She swung in Grandma's wooden swing that was tied to one limb of an almond tree. Then, Jane and Judy joined her and they swung higher and higher.

Pink-and-white flowers covered Grandma's oleander

trees, and her waterlilies had never been more beautiful. The waterlilies grew at the bottom of an old cistern. It was only a few feet deep, and three steps led down into it. Jackie sat on the middle step so that she could be closer to those lovely waterlilies. Some were lavender, some were white, and each was shaped like a star. Dark green leaves surrounded them, and these too were star-shaped. The plants had been brought over from the River Thames in England, and they were Grandma's pride and joy.

Jackie moved down to the third step and decided to pick the brightest waterlily she could find and take it to Mama. The lilies in the middle of the cistern were brighter and daintier than the ones near the steps. Jackie stretched a slender, sun-tanned arm as far as she could, so that she might pick the loveliest one. Her fingers touched the soft petals and she knew that in another moment she would hold it in her hand. But suddenly she heard a splash and felt the cold stale water cover her. Her feet touched the slippery bottom of the cistern, as her hand held tightly to the coveted waterlily. She picked it and stood for a moment admiring her prized possession. She would take it to Mama.

Jackie moved slowly through the dark water toward the steps. She felt something cold hit her shoulder, then her head. As she shook her head, a bumpy frog fell into the water. Then another one hit her and another. She was surrounded by frogs. She felt as if they were attacking her. She saw huge brown frogs with warts all over them, and wee green frogs with bulging eyes. They all felt cold and slimy. Jackie tried to walk faster to get away from them, but her feet refused to move.

"Mama help; somebody help me," she screamed.

Daddy and Mama came running and Daddy pulled her out while the frogs continued to jump all over her. They seemed angry that she dared invade their home.

"Thank goodness you're not hurt," said Mama.

"I'm not hurt, but I have frog footprints all over me," Jackie cried. "I know they are there, because I can feel them."

"Then we'll wash them off of you," Mama comforted her, and they walked toward the well.

"I have a present for you, Mama," Jackie said. She smiled while tears continued to trickle down her face. "Here is the waterlily I picked for you."

Mama held it as if she had just been given a priceless pearl. It was worth more to her than anything that money could buy.

"Indeed, it is the most gorgeous waterlily that I have ever seen," Mama replied. "Thank you for picking it just for me."

Mama poured a dipperful of cool water over Jackie, and Aunt Tes handed her a towel and one of her blouses. The blouse reached to her knees, and she wore it while Mama washed her dress and hung it on the line to dry.

Jackie ran outside to find her sisters. She found them walking on the old stone wall, arms outstretched as they inched their way along. Their hair was blowing loosely behind them. Jackie thought for a moment and decided not to join them, because soldier crabs lived in the old stone wall.

Soldiers are small land crabs that move in groups or families. They have a leader, and the others follow the leader. Looking like well-trained soldiers, they form a line and march from one place to another. That is why island people call them soldiers. A long time ago, one had bitten Jackie with its biggest claw and would not let go. She still had the scar on her hand, and it reminded her to stay away from soldiers.

She sat under a pine tree on the sun-baked earth and wondered what it was like when there were more houses around, and children playing everywhere, and no frogs.

Soon, Grandma called them to a delicious meal of baked beans and warm bread with guava jam. Jackie was sure that Grandma made the best baked beans in all the world.

"I'm sorry if I ruined your waterlilies, Grandma," Jackie said as they prepared to leave.

"There was no harm done," Grandma assured her. "The waterlilies will be just as lovely next week, and the grouchy old frogs will continue to make their home beneath them."

9

THE CALM BEFORE THE STORM

Mama held a pair of curtains to the window. All the curtains would need to be washed and ironed before she could hang them against the newly painted walls. She would need Washerwoman for one day just for washing and ironing curtains.

Jackie liked Washerwoman and she longed to know her name. However, when Jackie asked her name, Washerwoman just giggled and danced and said, "Not got no name." So the children called her Washerwoman. She came two days each week and washed clothes, but now Mama was thinking that maybe she could come tomorrow to wash the curtains.

"Hold off on the curtains for a few days," said Daddy. "There is an unsettled feeling about the weather. I feel it in the air. I don't like the looks of the sky."

The sun was setting, and as it sank low in the west, its rays sparkled and danced on the water. The sea looked as if it held all the diamonds of the world within it. Surely, Daddy was making a mistake, but of course, she did not tell him so.

Jackie wanted to feel closer to that sunset, so she crossed the street and sat on the rocky shore. The sky was beautiful. Motionless clouds looking like huge mounds of colourful cotton candy covered the sky, and here and there between them the blue showed through.

For sure, God loves beautiful things, because He made an island sunset.

Jackie watched as a mama seagull fed her babies. She left them in their nest in the big almond tree while she went in search of food. With her wide wings outstretched, she flew over the water until she saw a fish and then swooped down and picked it up in her beak. Her webbed feet pushed on the water, and she started her flight back to the nest. Jackie heard the baby birds chirp as they fought over their share of dinner. The mama seagull fed them well. She was a good mother.

And now it was time for the mama seagull to teach her babies to fly. They were old enough. She seemed in a hurry to teach them as she flew out of the nest and over the water. On her back was one little seagull. It looked scared, but Jackie knew that she could trust its mama to take care of her baby.

She had not flown far when she stopped and chirped to her baby, telling it what to do. The mama bird seemed to be falling, down, down, down, she went, but her baby was not on her back anymore. It was still high in the air flapping its little wings. Then the baby seagull began to fall, but just before it hit the water, its mama swooped down beneath her baby and put it once more on her back. That was the first lesson in flying. There would be a few more before the baby gull could fly safely by itself.

The mama bird taught the same lesson again, one

more time, then two, then three. At the end of the third time the baby seagull's little wings were strong and it could fly. A happy mama seagull flew back to her nest with her little one beside her. However, her work still was not done. She flew back over the water with another little bird, and then another, until she was sure that all three of her babies could fly. Afterwards she settled in her nest for a good night's sleep.

A fisherman sped by in his long canoe. His paddle barely moved as the canoe glided through the calm water. With a smile on his face and his straw hat pulled down to his eyes, he moved toward his fish-trap.

In the distance, Jackie saw a buoy that marked the spot where his fish-trap lay buried in the sea. The canoe stopped beside it. The fisherman leaned over the side of the canoe and pulled up the fish-trap. Jackie watched as several fish jumped while inside the fish-trap made of chicken-wire. She waited for the fisherman to take the fish out and lower the trap back into the water for tomorrow's catch. But instead, he picked up his paddle and paddled toward the shore. She had never seen a fisherman bring his fish-trap to shore before. Was it possible that he too suspected rough weather?

Jackie looked once more toward the sunset. The sun had gone down, and the water reflected the flame-tinted sky. She was still thinking that Daddy would be wrong this time. That sky could never tell of bad weather.

10

THE STORM

Before dawn, Jackie awoke. She heard a strange sound outside, as the wind whistled through the trees and heavy rain rattled like pebbles on the zinc roof. She walked to the window and looked outside. The banana trees bowed their long branches in the wind. One lone star sparkled in the sky while all the others slept. Jackie smiled as it winked at her. She was excited because she liked storms.

She went back to bed and tried to stay awake until morning, but her eyes blinked and she fell asleep. When she awoke, it was no longer raining, although the wind blew harder.

After breakfast, Jackie went outside to play in the back yard, and Jane and Judy joined her. Mama came to the door and told them to stay away from the coconut tree because coconuts had begun to fall. As the three sisters were trying to decide what to play, Old Smokey the stray cat came over the fence. His gray fur stood high on his back and he seemed angry. He was telling them something in his cat language.

"What's he saying, Jackie?" Jane asked. They all laughed. They always teased Jackie and told her that they knew she could speak cat language and bird language. And sometimes she almost believed that she could.

"I think he's saying that he doesn't like this weather. He only came to warn us that something strange is going on," Jackie replied.

"It's okay, Smokey, I'll give you something to eat," Mama told him, as she looked out the kitchen window. Jackie was sure that Mama could not understand cat language. She tempted him with meat and later with milk, but Old Smokey smelled it and refused to eat. He was insulted. He looked at Mama and said a few strange meows. He seemed to be telling her in simple language that he was capable of catching his own dinner. Still disgusted, he walked away.

The girls drew a hopscotch in the sand. They were hopping and skipping, and Jackie was winning. She wondered if they were allowing her to win or if she was winning fair and square. Sometimes it was difficult being the youngest sister. Anyway, she was trying to stay in the lead when Old Smokey jumped the fence once more. This time he had something in his mouth. He dropped it outside the kitchen door and called for Mama to come and see. It was a little bird, barely alive.

Mama looked out the door just in time to see Old Smokey as he walked around the bird in his usual proud manner. He saw her and said a few words, as he slapped at the bird to let her see that it was still alive. She could not praise him for eating a little bird, because she liked birds and she wanted him to eat mice instead. Finally, disgusted that no one praised him, he ate it. There was not one feather left to tell the tale. Then he licked his paws, washed his face, and yawned.

Daddy came from the printing shop and said he had heard the weather report on the radio. There was a storm to the northeast of Cayman, and it was moving in their direction. He looked worried. He probably was remembering the storm of 1932. That was the worst one to ever hit the island. Whenever someone talked about that storm, Mama put one finger against her lips to let them know that she would prefer they not talk about it with her children around.

Daddy and Mama had lived through many storms before, and they knew it was important for them to be prepared for it. So Mama took stock of the food in the kitchen. She made a list of the things she needed, and went across the street to the store to get them. Daddy put storm windows on the front of the house to cover the glass ones. The wooden windows on the sides and back of the house stayed on all the time. They hung on hinges and opened from one side, so they needed only to be nailed shut.

That evening, the wind blew furiously as the waves pounded the shore. The waves lashed beyond the rocks and moved under the big almond tree in back of the store. The three sisters crossed the street and stood under the almond tree. They giggled as a wave lapped against their bare feet and legs. Then the current pulled the water back and another wave hit them. They ran beyond the almond tree and stood on the rocky shore. Now the waves splashed and almost covered them. Their clothes were wet, but they did not care. The salt water trickled down their faces and stung their eyes, and they blinked often to soothe them.

Huge waves went higher and higher on the land. They had almost reached the store when Daddy called. He wanted Jane and Judy to help in the store because it was crowded with people as they prepared for the storm. Almost every customer held a bottle to buy kerosene from the big drum. Usually during a storm, the lights went out, and they lit kerosene lamps.

Jackie crossed the street and went home. Mama was trimming the wick on her kerosene lamp. The lampshade sparkled and the base of it was filled with kerosene.

"My goodness," Mama said, "you're soaked through and through. Get in the tub right now and get your bath." She took the black iron kettle from the back of the stove and poured hot water in with the cold. Mama said it was just enough to take the chill off.

Jackie put on her pajamas and ate supper. The baked chicken and rice was delicious, and the breadfruit salad was one of her favourites. Baw Baw made it the way she made potato salad, but she used breadfruit instead of potatoes. Since breadfruit is a vegetable, Jackie could never figure out why they called it breadfruit.

After supper, Mama took Jackie and little John on the porch and sat in the swing. She sang a lullaby to John as Jackie watched the storm intensify. She listened as Mama sang,

> *"Up, up in the sky, where the little birds fly,*
> *Down, down in the nest, where the little birds rest,*
> *With a wing on the left and a wing on the right*
> *We let the dear birds rest all the long night, "*

Just then, Daddy came in from the printing shop and said he had heard on the radio that the storm was worse and coming in their direction. He had a hammer in one hand and a bag of nails in the other.

"I might as well nail up the windows now, while I still can see to do so," he said to Mama. They heard pounding next door, and in the house in back of theirs, as neighbours tried to stay one step ahead of the storm.

When it was dark. Mama sent her three girls to bed. John was already asleep in his little bed. She and Daddy sat in the swing on the porch for a long time that night, with a watchful eye toward the troubled sea. All night long the wind howled and the waves beat against the shore. Jackie awoke during the night to that sound.

The next morning Daddy told them that the barometer was still falling, and he had a worried look on his face. It was the second day of the storm and the angry waves were so huge that they went across the street and into the front yard. Now Jackie understood why Daddy's father, Papa, had built the house and store on wooden stilts. If he had built them on the ground, the waves would have washed inside the store and the house.

Many trees fell and light poles went down. Chickens were blown from their roost in the trees. Daddy gathered them up and put them in the chicken coop, where they would be safe. Jackie was scared and decided that she probably did not like storms.

"If the storm gets a good bit worse, we'll all go inland where we'll be safe," said Daddy.

Finally, that night the storm passed the island. The radio reported that it had moved to the southwest of the Island of Grand Cayman. The barometer was rising slowly. The crisis was over.

Islanders could sleep now, but they would not know until tomorrow how much damage had been done. In the darkness they listened as big trees fell, but they were not sure which ones had fallen. Tomorrow they would know.

11

THE BIG ALMOND TREE

It was the morning of the third day of the storm. Jackie woke up and jumped out of bed. She had slept late and missed sitting in the kitchen with Mama and Daddy, but she saw them talking and shaking their heads as they stood on the porch. Jackie pulled on her clothes and joined them. The wind was quiet as it moved through the bare trees. Leaves had been ripped from the trees and lay lifeless and brown on the ground. A light rain fell, and the waves seemed tired. They no longer washed across the street.

Daddy was unaware that Jackie stood behind him as he talked to Mama in a low voice.

"There's destruction everywhere", said Daddy. "The wind blew Mr. Gullen's roof off, and a big tree fell across the street in the middle of town; but the big almond tree was probably the biggest tree to go down last night."

"The almond tree, did you say the big almond tree, Daddy?" Jackie asked. She looked toward the back of the store and saw her favourite tree on the ground. She started to cry and tried to run off the porch to go to it, but

Daddy caught her.

"It's all right, little Dupso," Daddy said. "We're blessed that it fell sideways. If that tree had fallen on the store, the store would have been gone also. We have much to be thankful for."

"But my friend lived in that tree," said Jackie. "The seagull and her babies had their nest in it." She told Daddy that the day before the storm, she had watched as the mama seagull taught her babies to fly.

"That's good," Daddy comforted her, "because now you can be sure that she took her babies and flew inland where they would be safe."

Jackie remembered that the seagull had seemed in a hurry that evening as she taught her babies to fly. She must have known even then that the storm was coming and that they would have to leave the nest.

The air smelled of the sea. Jackie usually liked that smell, but today it was strong. She looked down from the porch and saw the reason. Several fish lay lifeless in the yard. One tired sea crab crawled feebly up to the step. Daddy picked it up and threw it back into the sea.

Jackie went inside the house and played tic-tac-toe with Jane and Judy, trying to forget the storm. The rain had stopped but Mama said they should stay in the house until the sun came out to dry up some of the water.

Later that day, Daddy called his girls to help him outside. They were out the door in a minute.

"I want you to pick up the avocado pears that are on the ground," Daddy said. "They will ripen if we cover them with a blanket and keep them warm for a few days."

As he handed each girl a basket, he said,

I must not leave upon the ground
The food I cannot eat,
For many a little hungry one
Would think it quite a treat.

"Should we gather the naseberries also?" Jane asked.

"No, the naseberries are too little," replied Daddy. "We could not eat them."

Daddy gathered coconuts and breadfruits and stacked them in a heap on the ground. Then he picked up the dead fish with a shovel and put them in a pile. There was a conger eel among them. Daddy said it was six feet long if it was an inch.

The girls watched as Daddy cut the bones out of each fish. The bones he would throw away, but the meat of the fish he would bury in his garden. It would make fertilizer, and that way something good would come of the fish. They would not have died in vain.

While Daddy dug rows in his garden plot and buried fish, Jackie gathered seaweed that the storm had left behind. Daddy also used it for fertilizer. He buried the seaweed with the fish and smiled as he said, "Next spring, we should have the best garden ever."

Daddy's banana walk had been ruined by the storm. It was on a small piece of land a short distance from the yard. The big banana trees fell, but there was a new shoot beside each one. The storm had not hurt the small shoots, and soon they would be big trees. The biggest papaya trees went down also, but the smaller ones were left. Mama was happy about it. They all liked the ripe papaya fruit, and sometimes Baw Baw cooked green papaya with roast beef because the papaya tenderized the meat.

After the work was done, the girls crossed the street to see the big almond tree. It was bigger than they remembered. As Jackie reverently approached it, she thought of the time that she had climbed to the top. Her sisters had told her they could see across the island to the water on the other side from the top of that tree. Jackie decided she, too, wanted to see across the island.

She began climbing and she climbed and climbed. When halfway up the tree, she almost turned back, but then she kept on going up, up, up. She was almost to the top when she saw the red roof on the house on the other end of the island. Her sisters had mentioned that also. She climbed higher, and there in the distance was the water. She even saw two boats in the water.

While viewing the island from this great height, houses looked like match boxes in the distance. She saw the town with its rows of white buildings, and her eyes followed the buildings until she spotted the schoolhouse. Beside the schoolhouse was the familiar town clock, and a short distance from the town clock, she glimpsed her favourite guinup tree. Then she looked down at the ground and felt dizzy.

She moved slowly and carefully down the tree, as her hands held tightly to each branch. Finally her feet touched the ground. It was great to feel the sand under her bare feet and to know that she was safe.

But now that big almond tree had fallen. The waves washed the sand from around its roots, and the strong winds carried it down.

Suddenly Jackie remembered the seagull's nest. She searched first one branch and then another until she found it. The nest was still fastened to the branch. It was a good nest, but the mama seagull and her babies were not in it. They had flown to a safer home inland. Perhaps someday she would come back and build another nest in a nearby tree.

There were footsteps in back of Jackie, and as she turned around she saw Daddy. He had his own memories of the big almond tree. He had played in that tree when he was a boy, and his father, Papa, had told him stories of when he played in it as a child. As far back as anyone could remember, the big almond tree had always been there. One tear moved slowly down Daddy's face as he breathed a sigh.

12

PIRATES AND DUPPIES FOR HALLOWEEN

School vacation had ended, and the children were back in school. It was fun seeing old friends again and hearing the tales of summer. Jackie liked her new school uniforms. The dark blue jumpers and light blue blouses looked nice. She would try to take care of them. And nothing was better than new notebooks, all crisp and clean. She had vowed never to scribble on them and always to write neatly. But those vows had been made a few weeks earlier, and already the books were scribbled on and looked much like the ones they had replaced.

It was Halloween, and all over the schoolyard children told ghost stories. Island people have a special word for ghost. The word is "duppy". So the children giggled as they told duppy tales and pirate fables.

The bell rang, and the girls and boys formed a line and quietly filed inside. When the children were seated, the teacher stood before the class and told them to open their history books to England during the reign of Henry VIII. As Jackie turned the pages, she saw her new blotter. The front of the blotter was a picture of an old woman. She walked with a cane and wore a wedding gown. Beside her in a wheelchair was an old man. A poem beside them said:

> PROCRASTINATION—THE THIEF OF TIME
> The bride with white hair leans on her cane,
> Her uncertain footsteps need guiding,
> While along the church aisle with a toothless smile
> The groom in his wheelchair is gliding.
> Now who is this pair who so late are to wed?
> You'll find when you closely explore it
> That here is that rare and conservative pair
> Who have waited 'til they could afford it.

Jackie smiled and slipped it under her desk to Rita. She read it, laughed, and handed it to Molly. Soon the whole class had the giggles. Jackie was ashamed that she had started such an uproar. By the time the blotter had gone across the classroom, the teacher held out her hand. Jackie was scared. She felt sure that she was in trouble, and she had only meant to have a little fun.

Teacher looked at it and read it as she tried to keep from smiling. Finally she walked toward the door and her body was shaking. Could she be laughing? But when she turned around, her face was stern.

"Jackie, do not ever do that again," she said. She kept the blotter, but Jackie thought that was a small price to pay for the confusion she had caused.

After school, the children told duppy stories once more. Mama had told her girls never to believe a duppy tale. She said that there were no such things as duppies. Then Mama told her own duppy story and it went like this:

"One night long ago your grandfather was riding home on a horse," she said. "It was late at night and suddenly the horse stopped and refused to go on. Grandfather did everything he could to get the horse to go, but the stubborn horse stood still. Then, Grandfather saw what the horse was afraid of. There was a long light moving back and forth. He could not guess where such a bright light came from on a dark night. He had heard that a duppy would never allow a horse to go by it. Was this a duppy?"

"Grandfather tied his horse to a tree beside the road. With wobbly knees and a pounding heart he walked toward the moving light. As he got near it, he saw a palm tree which had a long branch covered with light bugs. The light bugs were only on the one branch, and it was blowing back and forth in the wind. Grandfather touched the branch and the light bugs flew elsewhere. Then he went back to the road, got on his horse, and went home."

"And that is why you should never believe a duppy story," Mama said.

When it was dark, the three sisters dressed in Halloween outfits and went across the street to the store. Jackie wore ragged clothes and an old straw hat, and tied noisy tin cans on her hands. She was a scarecrow. An ugly duppy came by the store with a sheet thrown over her head and two holes cut in it for eyes. She had a black scarf tied around her neck.

Blackbeard, the pirate, came by the store also. He wore a red plaid skirt and a black shirt. His high boots had silver buckles. A black patch was over one eye, held in place by a piece of elastic. In his hand he held a shovel.

"I'm going to dig for gold," he said. "I buried it on the beach last year. I need six brave people to help me dig."

"Not I," said the duppy, and "Not I," said the scarecrow, and "Not I" echoed voices around them.

"Then I'll dig for it myself," said Blackbeard, "and I won't share my gold with anyone." Then in a low voice they heard him say, "I had no intentions of sharing it with you anyhow. I'm a pirate, you know."

Black cats came by the store for candy, and witches appeared with long noses and broomsticks.

A bull stood a short distance from the store, and Daddy tried to give him candy but he refused. He stood stifflegged and still in the dark night. The pirate tried to guess who the bull might be.

"A bull's costume is a bit strange on Halloween night," said the pirate. "I'm sure there are two or three people under that costume."

They were amazed at how much he looked like a real live bull with horns curled upward. When they moved near him, he backed away. No amount of coaxing could get him to talk to them. They called him by every name they could think of.

"Tim, is that you?" said the witch.

"I think it's Brian," the black cat said. "Speak to me, Brian."

"Who would want to dress like a bull?" the pirate grumbled.

"You little boy, you little boy, could you tell me if you've seen a big brown bull anywhere?" a voice teased, as a slim figure moved bravely toward the bull.

"Moo, moo," bellowed the bull and everyone ran for shelter. He was a real live bull.

The pirate climbed the popnut tree, and the other Halloween creatures ran into the store where they would be safe.

"Sir, did you see a big brown bull go by here?" a man asked Daddy as he stepped in the store. "Our wildest bull tore down a fence and left the pasture," he continued. Three men were with him, and they all held lassos.

"He's headed north," Daddy replied. "He paid us a visit a few minutes ago."

"Thanks, bye," the men yelled as they hurried away.

13

WASHERWOMAN'S SONGS

Jackie made her bed and cleaned her room in a hurry because it was Saturday, and she wanted to run free in the sunshine and wind. She hoped that Mama would not ask her to do any more work.

"Mama, can I go out and play now?" asked Jackie.

"May I," Mama corrected her. "Yes, you may."

Jackie hopped and skipped as she ran toward Washerwoman, who was washing sheets, pillowcases, and towels.

"May I watch you for a while?" Jackie asked politely.

"Yes," Washerwoman answered, "sit under the tree and talk to me." She liked having the children around.

Washerwoman gathered sticks and piled them together on the sand. She lit them with a match, and the fire moved from one stick to another. Then she put the big caldron on the fire and filled it with water. Jackie had seen her put the clothes in boiling water many times before.

Over beside the breadfruit tree, on a tall wooden box,

she began filling the washtub with water. As she poured water in it, she sang this song,

Sing sail-ho, sing sail-ho, sing sail-ho, he cried
For the pirates are coming to rob us you know,
So he carried her to windward, the whole livelong day,
And he carried her to westward, but the ship would not stay.

She sang and danced as she put the clothes in the washtub. Then she put the scrub-board in the washtub also. Made of island wood, the scrub-board had ridges cut in it from the top to the bottom, with a bigger indentation at the top for the bar of soap. Washerwoman pulled one pillowcase up on the scrub-board, picked up the bar of brown soap, and moved it back and forth over the pillowcase. Then she took the pillowcase over to the caldron of boiling water and dropped it in. The fire crackled as she stirred the sticks. The water must be boiling or the clothes would not be clean.

She came back to the tub, lifted a sheet on the scrub-board, and put soap on it. As she walked back to the caldron, she picked up her big stick. It had been a broomstick at one time, but now she used it to push the clothes down in the caldron so that the water boiled over each piece of laundry. She continued singing, and Jackie sang with her.

"You like school?" she asked.

"Most of the time I do," Jackie replied.

"Well, study hard, my dear," she continued. "Eat plenty of fish heads. They will give you a good brain for learning."

Jackie smiled. She liked Washerwoman's tales. She

tried once more to get Washerwoman to tell her name. It was kind of a game that she played with the children.

"Not got no name," she said as she laughed and danced to her own singing. She was old, but she was happy. Her head was tied with a red bandana and her cotton dress was crisp and clean. She giggled as she sang, "Coconut water, is good for your daughter."

That song made Jackie thirsty. Before she could say anything Washerwoman picked two green coconuts, reached for a machete, and cut the husk away. She chopped the top off and handed one to Jackie. The other was hers. The coconut water was cool and refreshing, and Jackie ate the coconut cream that had just begun to form inside. It tasted like a soft, but chewy gel. She never got tired of eating green coconuts. Washerwoman finished hers and licked her lips.

"Mmmmmm, that sure was good," she said. She was ready to get back to work.

The clothes had been in the boiling water long enough. Once again Washerwoman picked up her stick and this time she lifted the clothes out of the caldron. Clouds of steam curled upward, as she dropped them into the washtub and waited for them to cool.

She tapped her foot and sang the calabash song.

> *Morning time, them wash them face*
>   *In a calabash*
> *Noonday time, them wash them clothes*
>   *In a calabash*
> *And in the evening time them wash them dish*
>   *In a calabash*

They both laughed. A calabash is a hollowed-out gourd, and Washerwoman often brought her calabash with her. She drank water from it, because the water tasted cooler on a hot day. But the song was a joke, because the calabash could never be used for the purposes mentioned in the song. It was not big enough. So they laughed every time she sang that song.

She scrubbed each piece of laundry until it was clean, and then she threw it into the rinse tub on the ground beside her. As her hand squeezed tightly on the blueing, tiny swirls of blue circled the rinse water. It gave the clothes a whiter, cleaner look. She rinsed each article, held it up and looked at it to be sure that she had done a good job. Then she hung it on the line to dry.

A mother hen went by with her brood of chicks, clucking as she gathered them beneath her wings.

"Your daddy got plenty of chickens now," Washerwoman said. "But you must not eat chicken on New Year's Day."

"Why not?" asked Jackie.

"Because if you eat chicken on New Year's Day, you'll scratch for a living the rest of the year." Washerwoman continued, "You should eat blackeye peas for good luck and green cabbage for money."

"I'll try to remember that," Jackie laughed.

Washerwoman invited Jackie to help her take the dry clothes from the lines. They were soft and clean and smelled fresh. She sprinkled the sheets and pillowcases with water, and folded and rolled each piece separately for ironing. Two black irons were on the back of the woodburning stove. Washerwoman knew when the irons were hot.

"If you spit on the iron and it sizzles, it's hot," she laughed. However, she thought that Mama would prefer that she used another method, so she shook a drop of water on the iron. It sizzled and the ironing began.

She ironed first one pillowcase and then another as she sang an island song.

> *"Mama look at Boo Boo," they shout.*
> *Their mother tell them,*
> *"Shut up your mout',*
> *That is your daddy."*
> *"Oh no, my daddy can't be ugly so."*

Jackie laughed and sang with her, and all too soon Washerwoman finished the ironing. Mama paid her and thanked her kindly, and she went home.

As Jackie helped Mama put the clothes away, she danced and sang.

"Goodness, I'm not sure I like you singing those Washerwoman songs," Mama said.

So Jackie quit singing them out loud, but she continued to dance, because Washerwoman's songs made her feel like dancing.

14

THE SAND HILL

After all the planning for Christmas, it seemed it never would get there. But finally Christmas was only two days away. Jane, Judy, and Jackie wrapped gifts and dreamed of the presents they would receive in return. Baby John unwrapped some gifts faster than the girls could put bows on them. Mama was baking fruitcakes. Daddy was making a list.

"Add Cousin Melinda to that list for me," Daddy said to Mama. "And we almost forgot Washerwoman."

Jackie was curious about Daddy's list, but it was a secret that he and Mama shared. Jackie could not figure out whether it was good or bad to be on Daddy's list.

"The truck is here with the sand," Judy yelled.

The girls ran to the porch and watched as two men shoveled sand out of the truck onto a sand hill in one corner of the yard. Soon the truck was empty, and Daddy thanked them and paid them.

The girls had scraped most of the old sand away, leaving the hard bare earth underneath, so the yard was ready to welcome the new sand from the beach.

Spreading the new sand was always fun and the girls looked forward to this pleasant chore each Christmas. It was as much a part of an island Christmas as Mama's fruitcake or Daddy's list.

Each girl got a thatch palm basket and sang a Christmas song as she walked toward the sand hill. Jackie was first to stand beside that enormous mound of sand. She told herself that perhaps it was a mountain instead of a sand hill and suddenly she wanted to climb to the top. She put one foot forward and then the other as she climbed higher and higher.

"I'm climbing a mountain," she sang, "and now I'm at the top of the mountain, and the world looks gorgeous from up here."

With outstretched arms, she enjoyed the thrill of knowing that she was at the top of her make-believe mountain. She was unaware that the sand hill was crumbling beneath her until she heard a voice.

"Jacqueline, get off that sand hill." It was Mama's voice, and she called her Jacqueline only when she was annoyed at her.

Jackie slid down the sand hill and stopped abruptly, sensing Mama's eyes still on her.

"I'm sorry, Mama. I didn't mean to climb it," she replied with eyes downcast. "I thought it looked like a mountain, and I wanted to stand at the top."

Jane and Judy filled their baskets and moved toward their chosen corner of the yard. Each girl worked from a different corner, emptying their baskets toward the middle of the yard. They emptied each load at just the right distance from the last.

Jackie tried to keep up the same pace as her sisters,

but they knew how to fill their baskets faster than she did, so their corners had more little mounds of sand.

Suddenly, she had an idea. She walked to the back of the house and pulled the old wheelbarrow out from where Daddy kept it. Then she found two buckets and put them in it, and she sang as she pushed it toward the sand hill. Perhaps now she could be the first to finish her corner. She filled her basket and the two buckets with sand and put them in the wheelbarrow, and smiled to herself as she moved toward her corner, emptying them in a row—one, two, three little sand mounds. It was a great idea.

But her sisters were whispering to each other. By the time she was back at the sand hill, they asked if they might take turns with the wheelbarrow, so they would all finish their work at the same time. They even told her that they would push her in it and give her a good wheelbarrow ride.

Old Smokey came over, inquisitive as usual. He said a few cat words to the partly diminished sand hill, and then he jumped in the wheelbarrow. Jackie sat beside him and her sisters pushed them. They were only walking at first, but then they started running. Faster and faster they ran as the old wheelbarrow squeaked and groaned. Old Smokey's back was hunched, and Jackie laughed so hard that she almost fell out. Then there was a shattering noise as the wheel rolled off of it. The tired old wheelbarrow came to a stop.

The girls giggled, but Old Smokey was angry, his eyes shooting flames. He spat and hissed at them and then he walked away.

Jackie picked up the wheel and her sisters helped her to pick up the wheelbarrow and put it back where Daddy kept it. She thought it best to wait until after Christmas to tell Daddy that they had broken the wheelbarrow. Perhaps, if he knew about it, he would write her name on his Christmas list. And what would Santa Claus think of her if he saw her name on that list?

The three girls agreed that was the right time to take a break, so they went inside the house to decorate the Christmas tree. The tree stood bare and alone in one corner of the living room. Daddy had cut it that morning from among the pine trees that grew close to the Seven-Mile Beach. Judy picked up the decorated pine cones and hung them on the tree. Jane looped long strands of curly beans from one branch to another. The red and black curly beans glittered between silver and gold tinsel. Jackie hung a plump Santa Claus with a white beard on one branch. He was carved from wood and his neatly painted red suit looked smart. Mama placed the gold star at the top. The Christmas tree was complete.

They went back to their work in the yard. By evening, the sand hill was gone. Hundreds of tiny sand mounds had replaced it.

"You've done a nice job," Mama said at supper. "You'll need to spread the sand tonight because tomorrow is Christmas Eve."

That night, as thousands of stars danced in the sky, the three sisters spread each little sand mound. They sang Christmas carols as they worked, smoothing the sand. When they had finished their work, they joined Mama and John in the swing and admired the beautiful white sandyard with the bright moonlight gleaming down on it.

"Oh, Mama, it looks like snow" Jackie said. "I'll

pretend that we have a white Christmas."

"Look toward the gate, girls," Mama replied.

Old Smokey had come back to guard it. He walked back and forth in front of the gate, his tail wagging, his eyes shining in the night. He knew that something unusual had happened that day and he wanted to feel that he was a part of it.

15

DADDY'S CHRISTMAS LIST

Jackie enjoyed her first glimpse of the sand yard as it glistened in the morning sunlight.

"Today is Christmas Eve," she yelled. "Hurrah, it's Christmas Eve." She would hurry and get ready to deliver the gifts to her friends.

Baw Baw's banana fritters smelled tempting, but Jackie could think only of Christmas. She sprinkled cinnamon and sugar on a plateful and felt full after only one bite.

With the gifts in the basket on the front of her bicycle, she began her exciting journey. Her legs pedaled faster and faster as she thought of the gifts she would receive. She stopped at Rita's house and handed her a gift.

"Merry Christmas, Rita," she said. Rita ran inside her house and returned with a gift for Jackie. Each girl shook her gift and tried to guess what was in it.

Rita got her bicycle and all her gifts and she and Jackie moved on toward Molly's house. On the way there, they met Molly and Tarla, so the four girls stopped their bicycles and exchanged gifts by the roadside. Then each girl started toward home.

"Mama, please may I open my gifts," Jackie asked as she ran inside the house. "Santa Claus is coming tonight and I'll have many gifts tomorrow.'"

"All right," Mama replied. "You may open them this evening."

"Thank you Mama—oh, thank you," Jackie said.

After dinner, Jackie swung in the hammock under the naseberry tree. The cool winter breeze whistled through the trees and rocked the hammock back and forth. Jackie had long ago forgotten the hot summer months. She fell asleep and dreamed of Daddy's list. She dreamed that it was a letter to Santa Claus, and the names that he had written on it were the people who treated him badly during the year.

When she awoke she told herself over and over that it was only a dream. She had never known Daddy to try to get even with anyone. She hoped that Santa Claus knew that she had been good, because she wanted many gifts.

"Add Mr. Spencer to that list," she heard Daddy say.

He stood by the kitchen door as he talked to Mama. Jackie thought that was a bit strange because Daddy liked Mr. Spencer. She was still remembering that dream.

"Please don't put my name on your list, Daddy," Jackie called. "I don't want my name on your list. I want Santa Claus to know that I've been a good girl."

"What's that all about?" Daddy asked. "I don't

know," replied Mama. They were laughing.

"Don't worry, I won't put your name on my list," Daddy assured her.

Jackie felt better. Now she could forget the dream. But while she was still swinging in the hammock, Cousin Melinda walked by the yard. Mama called to her and then handed her an envelope.

"Merry Christmas," Mama said.

"Thank you, and the same to you," Cousin Melinda replied. She held tightly to the envelope, and walked away.

Then, Mr. Spencer came to visit.

"I brought you a ripe sweetsop," he said to Daddy, as he handed him the tropical fruit.

"Thank you," said Daddy. "Thanks again, and have a nice Christmas." Daddy handed Mr. Spencer an envelope, and he held it to his heart as he smiled and walked away.

Jackie was puzzled. She had seen two people who were on Daddy's list receive a white envelope which made them happy. She wished that someone would open it in front of her, so that she could see what was inside.

That evening, Jackie opened the gifts from her friends. She received a pencil box from Tarla, crayons from Rita, and a blue ribbon from Molly. She was happy and excited.

"Now I'm going to deliver these," Daddy said. He held white envelopes in his hand.

When he came back, he handed one envelope to Mama.

"I didn't find Washerwoman," he said. "Give this to her when you see her."

Jackie wanted to sneak and open Washerwoman's envelope. But she remembered that Santa Claus was on his way, and he would know if she was good or bad.

That night, she hung her stocking beside the Christmas tree. Jane and Judy did not hang stockings. They said they were too big for Santa Claus to visit. But they wrote their names in large letters and put them under the tree.

Santa Claus was probably almost there. He was over the Caribbean Sea in his sleigh pulled by reindeer. By the next morning, he would visit every good little girl and boy on the island.

Jackie thought she would never get to sleep. But before long she heard people singing outside and she knew they were the carollers.

"Merry Christmas, everyone," Daddy and Mama said. Jackie jumped out of bed.

"Is this Christmas morning? Did Santa Claus fill my stocking?" she asked.

She put her hand in the stocking and pulled out a pretty gold ring with her birthstone in it. Then there was a bag of jacks and a ball and a box of marbles. Further down, she found bubble gum and a shiny red apple. She was happy. Then she looked under the tree and saw a lovely red dress with a white lace collar.

Jane found a watch by her name under the tree, as well as nail polish and a diary. Judy held up a bracelet with her name on it, a bottle of perfume, and a jewelry box. And they each had a gorgeous red dress.

John liked his boat and car, and he tried to eat all the bubble gum. Mama's eyes sparkled when she saw the necklace that Daddy gave her, and she liked the perfume from her three girls and John. Daddy opened his presents.

He got a blue necktie and a shirt.

"Hotdog," said Daddy. "This necktie matches my new shirt."

They were laughing when a voice said, "Merry Christmas, everyone."

"The same to you, Washerwoman," Mama said. She handed Washerwoman the envelope.

"Thank you, ma'am, thank you," Washerwoman said. She tore the envelope open right in front of Jackie's eyes. Money fell out of the envelope, and Washerwoman picked it up.

"Thank you," she said as she smiled and walked away.

At last, Jackie knew the secret of Daddy's list.

16

A FREE RIDE FOR OLD SMOKEY

Daddy was getting his garden plot ready for planting, so he took a day off from his printing to work in it. He mentioned at breakfast that he needed help with it. Jackie volunteered to be his helper because it was Saturday, and Jane and Judy worked in the store on Saturdays.

"Be ready to work hard, little Dupso," said Daddy.

When Jackie joined him in the garden, he was busy digging. He remarked that the soil was extra rich from the fish and seaweed he buried there after the storm. He said it was hard for him to wait to see what the rich soil would produce.

As Jackie turned the soil over on the other end of the garden, chickens flocked around her. They seemed inquisitive, as they walked around and scratched and pecked in the soil. It was almost impossible to keep them cooped up, since they had many chickens. A red dominica hen went by, making strange noises. Daddy said he was sure that her nest was nearby, but Baw Baw was unable to find it.

"I'll try to find it, Daddy," Jackie said. "I'll follow her around."

"That would be a job well done, if you find her nest," Daddy replied.

So Jackie left the garden and followed the hen. It was fun at first, kind of like playing detective. She hid from the hen and the hen hid from her. Jackie followed her past curly bean trees laden with red and black curly beans. They moved past oilnut trees, and Jackie picked an oilnut stalk with which to blow bubbles later. They went past and around papaya trees and banana trees, and still the hen kept going. Jackie realized that the hen was going round and round in a circle, and the wisdom of that old hen annoyed her.

She had almost decided to quit and forget it when suddenly the hen dashed under some bush and stayed there. Jackie peeped to see where she had gone and saw her nest with eight eggs in it. She put seven eggs in her skirt, left one in the nest for the hen, and whistled as she went home to show Daddy.

"Good for you," Daddy said, "you outsmarted the hen after all, didn't you?"

Jackie put the eggs in the kitchen and went back to work in the garden. She had scarcely begun her work again when a strange dog came to join them. He was as big as a young calf and Jackie was not sure she wanted to go near him. She only wanted a nice quiet day to work in the garden. It was usually peaceful out there, with woodpeckers pecking in the banana trees, ground doves scratching around them, and soft breezes blowing from over the sea. But today was filled with intruders, first the old hen and then the overgrown dog. She was wondering what would happen next.

Suddenly she heard a familiar sound and looked into the face of Old Smokey. Reminding her of a duppy, he seemed to come out of nowhere when she least expected him. Jackie waited to see what his mission was this time.

Old Smokey walked over to the huge dog and said a few polite meows. Jackie could almost hear him tell the dog that he was sorry, but he would have to leave. He walked round and round the huge dog, as if he were considering his size. The dog yawned and ignored Old Smokey and yawned again. But now Old Smokey was angry. He resented being ignored. He fussed and fumed at the dog, and his sharp teeth glistened in his open mouth.

Daddy winked at Jackie and whispered, "Be quiet. I think Old Smokey is going to teach him a lesson he'll never forget." So Jackie and Daddy quit work and just watched.

Old Smokey's eyes were wild. His one blue eye and one green eye never left the dog for a moment. He said some strange meows that they had never heard before. Jackie almost told him to please watch his language. Suddenly, the dog growled a slow, happy growl. Jackie was sure he was telling Old Smokey that he was not scared of a sassy little cat, because he was king of the territory. But that slow, happy growl was just too much. That insult was more than Old Smokey could take. He jumped high in the air and landed on the dog's back.

The dog was so scared that he began running as fast as he could with Old Smokey still hanging on. In his hurry to get away, he ran into the fence. The blow stunned the dog, but not old Smokey. His claws were secure in the dog's back. Finally, they went through the gate and headed down the road.

Daddy and Jackie laughed and laughed, and Daddy's gold tooth shined in the sun. They had just settled down to work in the garden when Old Smokey came back for his reward.

"Smokey, you're first class," Daddy said. "You're a good boy, Smokey."

Old Smokey liked Daddy to brag about him. He said some gentle meows, and Jackie was sure he told them that he could take care of dogs in fine style. Daddy and Jackie both agreed that he had a smile on his face.

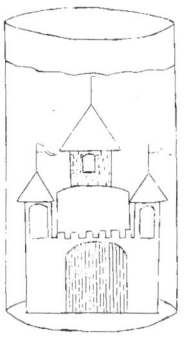

17

THE CASTLE

A full moon smiled at Jackie as she looked down at the calendar in front of her. She remembered what Washerwoman had told her one day as she washed clothes under the breadfruit tree.

"Good Friday is always the first Friday after the first full moon after the twenty-second day of March," Washerwoman had said. Jackie remembered those words as she looked at the calendar and realized that Washerwoman was right again. She liked Washerwoman's tales.

It was Good Friday, and Jane and Judy were in the kitchen getting three eggs from Baw Baw. Jackie joined them and they each got a glass and half-filled it with water. Then they each broke an egg and separated the white from the yolk. They gave the three egg yolks to

Baw Baw and each sister put the white of her egg into her glass of water. Plop, plop, plop went the egg whites as each girl dropped one into her own glass.

Jackie picked up her glass and walked toward the porch. Jane and Judy followed. They placed the glasses side by side on the porch rail and left them in the sun all day so that a design could form inside as the heat from the sun cooked the egg-white. That evening, they would see a picture inside each glass. Children all over Cayman did this on Good Friday.

Jackie was excited. Perhaps her glass would have a castle in it. That would mean that she would one day live in a magnificent castle and dress like a princess. Some island people believed that the design that formed in the glass told a story for the future. But Mama told her girls that an egg and water could not know what was going to happen.

When it was almost 12:00 noon, Jane, Judy, and Jackie left the glasses on the porch and walked over to Mrs. Rae's house. They asked if they might cut her bleeding-heart tree. Many children were standing around the tree, with its large heart-shaped leaves.

"When the clock says 12:00 noon, I'll give one of you a knife to cut it," Mrs. Rae said. They watched the clock and she handed Judy the knife.

"You may cut it now," she said.

Judy chopped into the tree with the big knife and sap poured out. The sap was not milk-white like it usually looked. Instead, it was red. Judy cut another part of the tree and crimson red liquid poured from it. The children gasped and put their hands over their mouths. They had cut it at other times during the year and the liquid that spurted out always looked like milk. But at 12:00 noon every Good Friday, the colour changed from milk-white to red. The sap that dripped from all bleeding-heart trees on the island on Good Friday was always red.

When they went home that day they asked Mama questions about the tree, but she had no explanation to offer them. As a little girl, she too had seen it happen every year.

Dinner was late that day and Baw Baw's mouth was in a pout. When she was angry, her mouth curled out and her eyes darted like arrows. She wanted the children to settle down and eat so that she could wash the dishes and go home. The turtle meat and rice was delicious, and with it they had baked plaintains and chewy cassava cake. Jackie ate the tasty dinner and wished she was a giant so that she could eat more and more of that turtle meat and rice.

That afternoon, Jane, Judy and Jackie swung in the swing on the porch. Tarla came over to visit them, and the three sisters ran to greet her. Her hand held tightly to a glass. The water in the glass had a white film over the top.

"Why does your glass look so strange?" Jackie asked.

"I did not have an egg," Tarla replied, "so I sprinkled powder in my glass."

"Well, that will never make a design," Jackie said. "Come with me to the kitchen."

They washed the glass, put water in it, and dropped an egg white in the water. They went back to the porch and put the glass in the sun. Then they swung in the swing, told stories and sang songs until evening.

As each girl walked toward her glass, she held her hands over her eyes and giggled. Jackie wanted to see what her glass would show. But she hesitated. Finally, each girl stood before her glass and shouted with delight.

"A Christmas tree," Jackie yelled. "Looky everybody, look at the Christmas tree and the big presents under it." It was the most beautiful Christmas tree she had ever seen. A tiny bubble was fastened to the top of the tree.

"A boat," Jane grinned. "I see a big boat in mine with many sails. I guess I'm going on a trip."

"A new bicycle," Judy shouted. "Look at this shiny bicycle with big wide tires. I'm so happy. I need a new bicycle."

"I don't know what mine is," Tarla said. "Somebody tell me what mine is."

The three sisters looked at Tarla's and shouted.

"A castle, yours is a castle," they shouted. It was gorgeous and just like the ones in story books. But Tarla's eyes were sad.

"I'm not sure I want a castle," she said. "Do you think that princesses are really happy?"

"I'll trade you, Tarla," Jackie said. "I'll give you my Christmas tree for your castle, because I want to be a princess."

Tarla looked once more at her glass. She saw the splendid castle with towers reaching upward to the sky. She had a choice now. She could keep her castle or trade it for a Christmas tree with many presents.

She made the decision and her eyes sparkled as she looked up at Jackie.

"I think I'll keep my castle," Tarla said.

18

NOT A YELLOWBIRD FALLS

Finally, the day came for Jackie to work in the store. She was standing in front of the mirror combing her hair when Daddy came in the house. He told her that he wanted her to spend one hour in the store so that the clerk could teach her what to do.

That was great news. She had waited a long time for this day. She continued to comb her hair and smoothed her thin summer dress as she asked Mama how she looked. Mama said that she looked just fine. Then she smiled and added: "But of course, I'm like the mama monkey who always thought that her little monkeys were the prettiest." They both laughed.

"Oh, Mama, I can't believe that I'm finally getting to work in the store," said Jackie. "Isn't that great?"

Mama agreed and told her to remember to be polite to the customers and to say "Thank you" to each one.

"I hope I'll remember, Mama, but what if I forget?" Jackie asked anxiously.

"I'm sure you'll do just fine," replied Mama.

Those words gave Jackie the courage to cross the street and step into the store. The big clock said 10:00 a.m. She hoped that the next hour would go by slowly. The nice clerk smiled and welcomed her. She asked if she would begin by feeding the little yellowbirds.

"Yes," Jackie said. The little yellowbirds were hungry and they were chattering in the popnut tree outside the window. Jackie looked at the shelf that was built on the outside of the south window. It had been built just for the little birds. She took a towel and wiped it clean. Then she reached into the big barrel of brown sugar, and lifted the scoop. As she walked to the window, Jackie thought she heard one little yellowbird telling another that breakfast was being served. On and on they told each other. By the time she had carefully spread the brown sugar over the shelf, there were hundreds of yellowbirds singing merrily.

She walked away from the window, and yellowbirds came out of the branches of the tree and covered the shelf as they ate. Jackie wished there were some way that she could count them.

A strange man stepped inside the door and asked if they would mind if he took pictures of the birds.

"Not at all, go right ahead," the clerk said.

He explained that he was writing an article about the island for a foreign magazine and the birds would brighten his story. Then he stood outside the window and took pictures.

Jackie looked at the birds as they hopped and sang, and she tried to remember a story that she had learned in Sunday School, about how God takes care of the birds. Her teacher said that not one of these little birds could fall to the ground without God's permission.

Mama often recited a verse about birds. She said it was overheard in an orchard and it went like this:

> *Said the Robin to the Sparrow,*
> *"I should really like to know*
> *Why these anxious human beings*
> *Rush about and worry so. "*
>
> *Said the Sparrow to the Robin,*
> *"Friend, I think that it must be*
> *That they have no Heavenly Father*
> *Such as cares for you and me."*

Someone spoke and Jackie turned her head.

"I want threepence worth of brown sugar, sixpence worth of flour, and threepence worth of lard," a lady said.

The clerk looked at Jackie as she told her what to do.

"That will be a pound of brown sugar, two pounds of flour, and half a pound of lard. Be sure to put the lard on wax paper when you weigh it."

The brown sugar held just right in a one-pound paper bag, but a two-pound bag was a wee bit small for two pounds of flour, so Jackie put it in a three-pound bag and folded the top over so that it would not spill. The lard was messy to weigh, but finally she got it wrapped.

"Anything else, please?" asked Jackie.

"No, I don't think so," the lady replied.

"Then that will be one shilling, ma'am," Jackie said. The lady held tightly to a piece of brown paper in her hand. As she unfolded the paper, Jackie saw money in it. She handed Jackie one shilling for the groceries, picked them up, and walked out the door.

Jackie heard noises in back of the store. She walked to the back door and looked out. Tibby was sawing a branch off of the big almond tree. Now that the tree was dry, it provided many families with firewood. With her wheelbarrow beside her, Tibby mumbled to herself. Swish-swish went her saw as her arm moved back and forth. Once she looked up, smiled with Jackie, and said "I'm doing my best."

Jackie walked toward the counter as a customer stepped in the store. "I would like a penny worth of paradise plums," a small voice said, as a little hand reached over the counter. Jackie wrapped four paradise plums, and as she reached over the counter to put them into the small hand, she saw that it was little Rob, who lived down the street. His face was round, and freckles were sprinkled across his nose and cheeks. His sandy, curly hair was bleached by the tropical sun, and his emerald-green eyes twinkled when he smiled. In his hand was a silver threepence.

Jackie pulled the money drawer open and took out two big copper pennies and gave him his change.

Suddenly, the big clock chimed. It was 11:00 a.m. She thanked the clerk for the things she had taught her. Then she walked over to tell the yellowbirds goodbye, but she was surprised when she looked down at the shelf. They were gone. They had eaten until they were full and then had flown away.

Jackie put a paradise plum in her mouth. It was her favourite candy. Daddy had ordered them from England. As she crossed the street again, anxious to tell Mama about her morning, she knew that she had learned her best lesson that day, not from the kind clerk or customers, but from the little yellowbirds. She was remembering that God fed them every day and that not one of those little yellowbirds would fall to the ground without Him knowing it.

19

WHERE SEA BREEZES BLOW

Jackie sat on the rocky shore and watched the sunset. A mama seagull chirped in the popnut tree as her babies fought over the fish that she fed them. This was Jackie's friend, the seagull who had lived in the big almond tree the summer before.

Waves rippled gently against the shore as goggle-eyed fish chased tiny sprats. Jackie watched as the sprats jumped out of the water. Far in the distance, a huge ship looked like a wee toy on the horizon as it passed the island. The soft sea breeze blew Jackie's hair in her eyes and she pulled it back in place with a barrette. As the tiny waves lapped against the rocks, Jackie remembered that only that morning those waves had been strong enough to break a ship in two as they beat violently against it.

There was a storm nearby, and even though it had not hit the Island of Grand Cayman, it had left a path of destruction. The night before, a ship pulled into the harbour, trying to find a refuge from the storm. The captain had watched as the light from the lighthouse welcomed him, and he steered toward land. That morning, the strange ship was in the harbour.

"That ship is in trouble," Daddy said. "It looks like it went ashore during the night."

All that morning, the angry waves poured against the ship as the stern swayed back and forth under the pressure. The front of the ship was stuck in the sand at the bottom of the sea. Jackie watched as boats tried to pull it to safety. Smaller boats hooked huge chains to the ship and tried to pull it backwards, but to no avail.

Jackie got Daddy's binoculars and put them to her eyes as she traced every detail of the old ship with rust spots on its side. It was the biggest ship that she had ever seen. She caught a glimpse of the ship's name. Big letters on the side spelled *Calle*.

That afternoon, the captain and crew left the ship, because all efforts to save it had been in vain. As the wind shifted, the waves continued to lash against it. Then Jackie heard a loud cracking sound and a crunching noise as the ship broke in two. Thick black smoke and red flames curled upward toward the sky. The ship was on fire. The fire raged for what seemed like a long time after the ship broke in two.

Suddenly Jackie heard a voice singing,

> *Calle burning, Calle burning,*
> *Look yonder, look yonder,*
> *Fire-fire, fire-fire,*
> *And we have no water.*

Washerwoman was singing as tears streamed down her face.

"It's all right, Washerwoman," Jackie said. "The

captain and crew are safe. There's no one left on board."

"But it was so beautiful," Washerwoman replied.

Jackie had never thought that the ship was beautiful. She saw that it was black and rusty and probably had been through many storms. But Washerwoman insisted that it was beautiful.

Now, as Jackie looked once more toward the strange smokestack protruding from the sea, she knew that it was the only visible evidence of the huge ship that had gone down that afternoon.

In only a few short hours, the waves were calm and looked like a picture of gentle playfulness. Jackie felt that she knew the sea well, but she could never predict its actions from one day to the next. She looked back toward the sunset just in time to see the sun, in all its glory, disappear on the horizon as if etched by an artist's hand.

As Jackie crossed the street and went home, she felt happy that she was an island girl, and lived where sea breezes blew. She was thankful that she had a sweet Mama and that Daddy had a gold tooth that glistened in the sun. And she liked her sisters and baby brother. That night as they sat on the porch, she felt content and secure.

"Daddy, guess what," Jackie said. "The tiny sprats are going to be happy to have the *Calle* under the water so that they can hide from bigger fish. That old ship will make a safe home for sprats, won't it, Daddy?"

"Yes, it will," replied Daddy.

"And Mama, guess what else," Jackie continued. "The mama seagull is back and she has built her nest in the popnut tree, and she has more baby seagulls. Isn't that great?"

"Yes, it is," Mama said. "And soon you will be able to watch the mama seagull teach her babies to fly."

Mama was humming to herself. "Girls, would you like to sing with me?" Mama asked.

Their voices blended as they sang the beautiful song that Mrs. Leila Ross Shier had composed. Many years later, it became the Islands' National Song.

"BELOVED ISLE, CAYMAN"

O land of soft, fresh breezes, of verdant trees so fair,
With Thy Creator's glory reflected ev'rywhere.
O sea of palest em'rald, merging to darkest blue,
Whene'er my thoughts fly Godward, I always think of you.

CHORUS
Dear verdant island, set in blue Caribbean Sea,
I'm coming, coming very soon, O beauteous isle, to thee.
Although I wandered far, My heart enshrines thee yet
Homeland fair Cayman Isle, I cannot thee forget.
Away from noise of cities, their fret and calking care,
With moonbeams' soft caresses, unchecked by garish glare.
Thy fruit with rarest juices, abundant, rich, and free,
When sweet churchbells are chiming, my fond heart
    yearns for thee.

When tired of all excitement, and glam'rous worldly care,
How sweet thy shores to reach, and find a welcome there.
And when comes on the season, of peace, goodwill to man,
'Tis then I love thee best of all, Beloved Isle Cayman.

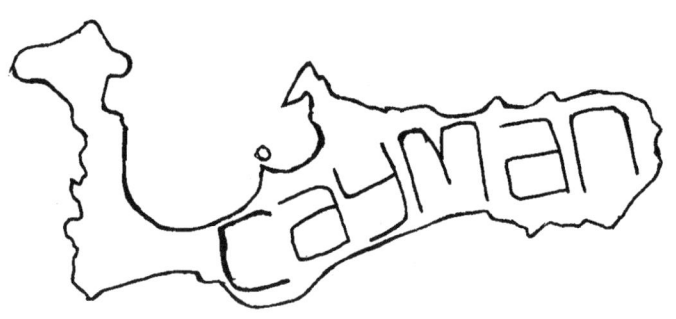

BY THE SEASHORE OF CAYMAN

By
Jackie Bodden

Illustrated by Susan Acree

CONTENTS

1. SHOES FOR AN ISLAND PRINCESS — 103
2. GO BULL GO — 109
3. THE LITTLE HOUSE UNDER THE TANGERINE TREE — 115
4. AN EASTER TO REMEMBER — 122
5. THE FORBIDDEN MANGO — 129
6. A LOOK INSIDE THE CISTERN — 136
7. THE EMPTY CISTERN — 142
8. THE INVISIBLE LOBSTER — 147
9. A PIRATE'S TREASURE — 155
10. THE SECONDHAND COFFIN — 163
11. IF ONLY DUPPIES COULD PINCH — 169
12. ISLAND DOCTOR — 174
13. THE SHIP BENEATH THE SEA — 180
14. SHE'S NOT OLD — 187

*To My Husband
With Love*

1

SHOES FOR AN ISLAND PRINCESS

"Mama," Jane said, "I've lost my new shoes. My costume is all ready for the concert tonight, but I can't find my shoes."

"Goodness," Mama said, "they can't be far. We just bought them two weeks ago."

Tears streamed down Jane's face. "What'll I do. We can't buy any more. It was just luck we found those to fit."

"Well, don't panic. They'll turn up."

Jackie put her hands over her ears and hurried toward the front porch. She didn't want to think about it. She would rock in the swing. She would listen to Daddy printing in the printing shop that he had built next to the house. She would watch the customers go in and out of Daddy's store across the street. The little gray store looked all lonely, sitting off by itself, next to the rocky shore and the sea.

She could still hear the panic in her older sister's voice as she asked Baw Baw, "Have you seen my shoes?"

"No." Baw Baw told her. "I don't come in the house long enough to see your shoes. I'm always too busy cooking."

Judy rode up on her blue bicycle with the big fat tires. She leaned it against the porch and ran inside. She too was older than Jackie, but Jackie's legs were longer.

"My shoes!" Jane told her. "Have you seen my new shoes? The concert is tonight and they're missing."

"I haven't seen them since the day Mama bought them, but we have to find them. They looked so right for your princess costume, with their clear plastic heels and all."

Jackie thought it seemed strange that no one asked her about the shoes. She left the porch and ran toward the back yard.

John played with his plane, beneath the sweetsop tree. He had scraped the sand away and made an airstrip. Vroom, vroom went the airplane as he wound the key and released it to taxi down the pretend runway.

Washerwoman was washing clothes on a scrub-board under the big breadfruit tree.

"My-oh-my, but you're in a hurry today. Stop and sing with me."

"Not today," Jackie said, and she kept on running. She didn't stop until she was beside the pear tree in a corner of the back yard. Sliding one hand into the hollow trunk of the old tree, she pulled out her beloved costume.

Jackie slipped Mama's dress over her head and smoothed it as it swept to the ground. *Oh, how elegant she must look! So grown-up,* she thought, in *Mama's castaway satin gown.* She would practice her part again.

She had written a play and had practiced it for weeks. She was ready to present it, but everybody that she invited was busy. She had even offered free lemonade. But still nobody came to watch her.

Strange, Jackie thought. *Now they were all excited about going to a concert in the Town Hall to see Jane act as a princess.*

Slowly she reached back inside the hollow tree trunk and this time she pulled out her precious shoes. She smoothed her hand over the blue suede straps, and slipped them onto her feet. They fit perfectly. She was a princess, but nobody seemed to care.

Far in the distance, she could hear the panic. She watched as Daddy left the printing shop and walked quickly to the house. She knew that he would buy Jane more shoes if he could, but there were none to buy.

Washerwoman walked toward Jackie, her head tied with a red bandana.

"I come to watch your concert," she said.

"Oh, good," Jackie said. She slipped the cardboard crown on her head and hid behind the pear tree.

Washerwoman sat in the shade of a tree sipping coconut water from her calabash. She watched as Jackie walked out on her pretend sandyard stage and curtsied. Then she began to sing and dance, and Washerwoman tapped her foot and sang with her:

> *After the ball was over,*
> *After the break of dawn,*
> *After the dancers leaving,*
> *After the stars had gone.*

Many a heart was breaking,
If you could see them all.
Many the hopes that had vanished
After the ball.

Washerwoman clapped her hands and smiled her beautiful smile. It didn't matter that she was snaggletoothed or old.

"You did good," she told Jackie. "You look just like a real princess. Now you can sing that song better than Washerwoman."

Jackie was beaming because someone liked her show! She curtsied again before leaving her imaginary stage to disappear behind the pear tree.

"Jackie." Mama called. She was scared. She pretended not to hear.

"Jacqueline, come here right now!" Mama said. Jackie ran as fast as she could. When she reached the back door, she lifted her skirt slightly, like she had seen Mama do when she stepped up with a long skirt.

"My shoes." Jane gasped, pointing to Jackie's feet. "Take them off right now. You're getting them all dirty!"

Jackie burst into tears and reached down and slipped them from her feet.

"Oh, Mama, they've shrunk! They can't fit me anymore," Jane said.

She handed them to her, and Mama's face turned red.

"What have you done to her shoes?" Mama asked, throwing them to the ground.

"I cut the straps off and nailed them to the soles of an old pair of my shoes, Mama. I needed them for my costume."

"Your costume for what?" Mama asked.

"For my concert," Jackie told her. "I'm a princess in it, but nobody had time to watch me. Nobody, except Washerwoman."

"What'll I do?" Mama asked, glancing sideways at Daddy. "They were so perfect for her costume."

"Nothing in life is ever perfect!" Daddy said.

Mama pulled off her slipper and Jackie closed her eyes as she waited for her spanking. Then she felt an arm go around her shoulder. It was Daddy's arm.

"What you did was wrong. Dead wrong," Daddy said. "But you'll not be spanked for it. Daddy is sorry that he told you he didn't have time to watch your concert before. But he has time now. Will you invite me once more?"

2

GO BULL GO

"I'm worried about Sally," Mama told Daddy as they sat by the kitchen door watching the sun peep over the distant trees.

"She's probably okay," Daddy told her. "You know, Sally comes and goes at her own pace."

"That's true," Mama said.

Later Jackie's long legs hurried down the footpath toward Sally's tiny house. Faster and faster she ran, her skirt flying behind her. Soon she was there, but Sally was nowhere in sight. A large stick leaned against her door to keep it shut.

Jackie glanced up at the tamarind tree that grew near Sally's house. Looking like long, brown, knobby fingers, the tamarinds hung in clusters from the branches. Jackie grabbed a handful from a low branch. Outer shells crunched and separated from the sour-sweet fruit covering the marble-size seeds. She felt her jaws tingle, and she winced from the taste.

"Want to go with me to shake ripe mangoes from the big mango tree?" a voice asked.

Lil Go-Go moved toward her with a thatch basket on her arm.

"Sure," Jackie told her. "Which tree?"

"The one in Mr. Toshy's grass-piece," Lil Go-Go said.

"Oh, no," Jackie said. "Mama warned me about the cows in that cow pasture."

"Okay," Lil Go-Go said. "Then I'll go alone," and she walked away.

Jackie caught up with her and they skipped happily toward the big mango tree.

"Looky, ripe mangoes!" Lil Go-Go said. "The tree is loaded with ripe mangoes."

As Jackie crawled between the barbed wire fence, she saw the cows. In a far corner of the pasture, four cows grazed amidst the tall grass. They looked harmless enough as the two girls ran toward the mango tree.

"Don't shake it," Jackie told her as they climbed the tree. "We'll handpick the mangoes and your basket will be full in no time at all. Then we can leave."

When the basket was full, they hung it on a limb and began eating. Jackie sat on a branch, kicking her feet back and forth, eating a sweet, juicy mango. Then the two girls told stories and Lil Go-Go sang:

> *Mangoes hanging from trees, girl.*
> *Mangoes hanging from trees,*
> *Take a look at those cows, girl.*
> *Cows would you stay there, please?*

"Sing some more," Jackie told her, and the girls laughed and sang it again. Then, from the corner of her eye Jackie saw something move.

"There's a bull coming toward us."

"You're teasing me, right?" Lil Go-Go said and she began singing again.

"No. Be quiet. Don't move," Jackie told her.

"Moo-oo-oo!" the bull bellowed. "Moo-oo-oo." He scared Lil Go-Go and she dropped a mango seed. It hit him between the eyes. The slippery seed stuck to the bull's forehead. He shook his head but the seed didn't budge. Lil Go-Go and Jackie giggled softly.

Suddenly he charged toward the trunk of the tree and rocked it with his horns. Mangoes hit the ground like rain. Goose bumps rose on Jackie's arms and the back of her neck. "Oh, no! He's trying to uproot the tree."

From her branch on the other side, Lil Go-Go finished eating her mango, but she was afraid to throw away the seed, so she put it in her basket.

The bull ranted and raved. Jackie thought for sure that he would get tired and go away, but he just bellowed louder.

The girls sat still not daring to move. Then Jackie heard a cracking noise and felt herself fall. Her summer dress caught on a branch and she hung in midair. Her tired arm still clung to the branch above her.

"Help. Somebody help!" Jackie screamed. "Get me out of here."

"Don't move," a voice said. It was Baw Baw. She stood beside the barbed wire fence and threw sticks at the bull.

"Go, bull, go!" Baw Baw yelled. "Get away from here." Finally, he ran toward the cows in the corner of the pasture.

Jackie pulled her dress loose from the branch. She jumped down and yelped as her feet hit the rocky ground below. In her haste to escape she ran into a cow-itch tree. Now itchy fuzz stuck to her, and the wind blew it toward Baw Baw. Arms waved in an effort to stop the floating cow-itch fuzz. She scratched her neck and face and jerked Jackie under the fence.

Baw Baw reached down and picked a handful of broomweed. "Get yourself home, Lil Go-Go," she said, and she shook the broomweed at her. Then she turned to Jackie. "I declare, you're wilder than any critter! I'm taking you home to your mother."

"I'm okay now. Thanks for chasing the bull away. You don't need to take me home."

"Yes, I do," Baw Baw said. "Girl, you ought to be ashamed of yourself, worrying your mama like this. She couldn't even eat, she was so worried about you. If she had the patience of Job you would wear it out."

Baw Baw held tightly to Jackie's hand and tugged her along. As she fussed she switched Jackie's legs, and the broomweed stung and she cried. And all the while, Jackie scratched as the cow-itch fuzz spread over her.

Finally, they were home, and Baw Baw told Mama all about it. Mama's face turned red and little lines formed around her mouth.

"I'm sure you did a good job chasing the bull away, and I'm grateful," Mama said. She was looking at the red marks on Jackie's legs.

"I switched the mosquitoes off her," Baw Baw said.

"I see," Mama replied.

Baw Baw left for home and Mama said, "I think you've been punished enough. You've probably learned your lesson. However, since you can't be trusted to stay away from cows and cow-itch, we'll have to think of something that will keep you near to home so I can watch you."

Mama said nothing while Jackie ate the fish cooked in coconut milk and breadfruit and cornmeal dumplings.

Then she put first one item and then another on the table. There was a tiny frying pan and a little pot, two tiny plates and a couple of old forks and knives and a tin cup.

"I want you to build a little house to play in," Mama said.

"Okay," Jackie said and she reached up and hugged her.

That night Jackie lay in her bed beneath the screened window. She heard the sea splash against the shore, and she watched the breadfruit leaves sway in the breeze. She thought of the nice little house that she would build. She would catch fish to cook, if Mama would trust her to fish from the sharp, jagged iron-shore in back of the store.

And best of all, it would be safe under a nearby tree, far away from bulls, and cow-itch trees.

3

THE LITTLE HOUSE UNDER THE TANGERINE TREE

Jackie had begun clearing a spot beneath the naseberry tree in one corner of her back yard. She thought she might like to build her little house in its shade.

Her friend April skipped down the footpath just beyond the fence. "What are you doing?" April asked.

"I'm going to build a little house to play in and Mama might even allow me to cook in it. See, I have plates and forks and pots."

"Sounds like fun. I've been wanting to build a house too," April said. "Will you come with me to ask my Mom if I can help you build it?"

Jackie climbed the fence, and she and April ran along the footpath toward April's house. As she looked back, Mama waved to her from the kitchen window.

April's twin sister Kim met them in the yard. They told her what they had planned to do.

"I know the perfect place for a little house," Kim said.

"Tell us where," the girls chimed.

"Under our tangerine tree. It's a good shade tree but it's never borne tangerines." The girls skipped toward it. Jackie had never really noticed it before.

"See, its leaves have turned from green to black," Kim said. "Mom says it's got tree lice."

Jackie covered her mouth with her hand and stepped back.

"Can't catch it, silly. Unless you're a tree," April said. They all laughed.

When April told her mom about it, she said, "I see no reason why you shouldn't build it there."

Kim wasn't real excited about it, but April and Jackie were ecstatic.

Every weed was pulled from the ground beneath the tangerine tree. They made a broom from broomweed and swept the sand. Soon they laid the foundation for their house. Four posts stood in place, one for each corner. Four pieces of wood were nailed across the tops.

April and Jackie gathered big sticks and little sticks and thatch leaves from the thatch palm trees. They collected pieces of plywood and nails, thatch string and cardboard.

Soon they had the foundation for the roof completed, with many sticks crisscrossed and tied securely in place only a short distance apart.

"I'm ready for you to hand me the thatch palm leaves," Jackie said, as she perched atop a wooden crate and held thatch string between her teeth.

"Here goes," April said. "Here is the first thatch palm leaf to build our roof." She handed it to Jackie, who pulled a thatch string from her mouth and tied it in place. When a row of thatch leaves had been tied to the highest stick, Jackie moved on to the stick beneath it. She and April took turns overlapping the previous leaves with a new row of thatch leaves, until several days later the roof was completed.

April and Jackie sat inside their little house without walls and admired it.

"It's a neat house," April said. "Not one fleck of light can be seen shining through that green roof."

"It will keep out the sun and rain, but we still have no sides," Jackie said.

"We'll think of something," April told her.

Every morning now, Jackie jumped out of bed and hurried to join April.

"I need never wonder where Jackie is anymore," Mama said one morning. "That house has captured her heart."

Before long, the cardboard sides were held in place with thumbtacks. The house was completed. There were no windows, but the front of the house was left open to let in the sunlight. Jackie folded a piece of crocus sack and placed it in a corner to cover the opening in case of rain.

One by one, friends dropped by to see the house.

"We shouldn't let just anyone into our house. Some are just plain nosy," April said. "What do you suggest we do about it?"

"We could think of a password and only allow the people who guess it to come in," Jackie said.

"Good idea! Let's pick a word that they will have a hard time guessing. How about Periwinkle?"

"Seashell?"

"Curly Beans?"

"Skilly-pots?"

Then April reached down and picked up something that sparkled in the sun. A small piece of broken blue glass. Her eyes lit up as she said, "BlueSparkle?"

"BlueSparkle it is," Jackie said. "Good name."

"Now that all that is over," April said, "tomorrow we'll furnish our house."

"Sounds good!"

The next morning Jackie arrived with the housewares that Mama had given her. April added a mug for lemonade or water and bowls and a wooden box to hold their precious dishes and silverware. This they kept in the far corner of the house.

Kim came by, and April told her to guess the password so she could come in. After ten guesses she was allowed to enter anyway. Kim placed three empty tin cans on the ground. She gathered twigs and laid them between the cans. Then she set the small pot on them.

"This is our stove," she said. "Now, what do we cook?"

"Let's go fishing!" April said.

Jackie stopped by the house and asked Mama's permission. "Be careful, girls," Mama said.

The three girls tied fishhooks to twine and picked some whelks from the shore for bait.

"Let's fish from the point where the shore ends behind Daddy's store," Jackie said. "Out there the water is deep and there are lots of fish."

It wasn't long before a red grunt picked at Jackie's line. He swallowed the bait, hook, and all, and she pulled him to shore.

"Look, everybody. I caught a fish, I caught a fish," she said. "How do I get him off the line. Somebody help me." The fish wiggled and tossed.

"Hold still," Kim said, "and I'll take the hook out of his mouth."

"Throw him back," April said. "He's gonna die."

"You bet he's gonna die," Jackie told her. "We're gonna eat him."

Then Kim caught a yellowtail fish, and April caught another red grunt.

The girls cleaned the fish and washed them in the sea. They pierced their mouths and slipped thatch string through the holes. Then they tied them together, like they had seen fishermen do. Swinging them back and forth, they went by to show Mama.

"Good for you," Mama said. "They will make a nice meal." She gave them ripe plantain and three big rolls that Baw Baw had baked that day.

The girls rushed to show April and Kim's mom what they had caught. "I've got hot pepper sauce that will taste great on the fish and mango jam for the rolls. But I'm warning you girls, you must never cook without my supervision." She told them. Then she handed them the bottles of pepper sauce and the mango jam. Three happy girls skipped away to their little house to cook their first meal.

"Salt and pepper the fish, April," Kim said. She had lit the twigs and was fanning them with a big grape leaf to keep the fire alive. Jackie peeled the plantain and sliced it. She put oil in the frying pan and placed it on the fire. When the oil was hot she fried the plantain first, then the fish, the way Baw Baw did. She looked up and April and Kims' mom stood just outside the little house, watching every move the girls made.

During that summer, much food was cooked in that little house. Trails of smoke seeped through the thatch roof and among the branches and the leaves of the tangerine tree. Gradually, the leaves changed from black to green, and one day white flowers covered it.

Kim and April called to their mom to come and see, and she smiled as she looked at the tree.

"It's a sight to behold," their mom said. "The smoke from your cooking has healed the tangerine tree, and soon you girls will be eating tangerines from your own back yard."

4

AN EASTER TO REMEMBER

"Eat your Easter bun and cheese so you can get ready for church," Daddy told Jackie.

"I don't want to go. I like Sunday School better. Anyway, my nose hurts."

Daddy put his remaining piece of Easter bun on his plate and pushed it away from him.

"Come here and let me see your nose," Daddy told her.

Jackie walked across the dining room to where Daddy sat at the head of the table. She covered her nose with her hand to hide it, but Daddy gently moved it away.

"I know it hurts," he said, "but it will heal. I just wish there was a visiting surgeon here now that we could take you to. But your mother did a good job of pulling it back in shape. The worst part now is the bruise where the blood drained and settled."

"So can I stay home?" Jackie asked.

"No," Daddy said. "There would be no one here to leave you with, and anyway, it is Easter Sunday."

Jackie got dressed in the frilly white Easter dress that Mama had made for her. As she looked in the mirror, she thought how pretty her dress was with the pink satin bow and little pink forget-me-nots on the side.

It was too bad her nose ruined her outfit. Mama had warned her not to climb high in the hammock the previous day as she and John played seesaw. And in her heart, she hadn't meant to.

But now she remembered inching her way higher and higher toward the rope that was tied to the hammock. She recalled the hammock tilting, and hitting the floor face down. When she stood and looked in the mirror, she saw that her nose had been pushed to one side of her face.

After that, she only remembered Mama crying, as she time and again rinsed a washrag and squeezed Jackie's nose. When finally it stopped bleeding, Mama examined it.

"I think it's going to be okay," she said. "It looks like I squeezed it back in place."

Jackie was thankful that John had not fallen from the hammock. He was still in it, holding to the sides.

When finally they were in church, Jackie wiggled in the pew and played with Mama's accordion fan. Her sleeves felt tight, and her petticoat, with its layers of starched frills, itched her legs. Mama elbowed her each time she wiggled, and Jackie could feel Mama watching her.

Jane sat beside Jackie in her Easter dress with the green ribbon, and she listened to every word the preacher said. She held tightly to the Bible in her lap. Jackie wished she could be good like Jane. Mama could trust her to sit at the end of the pew because she never had to elbow her to get her to behave.

Little brother John sat on the other side between Mama and Daddy, and Judy was at that end of the pew. She looked across at Jackie and smiled and Jackie thought she was trying to say, "It's okay, I know just how you feel."

When Mr. Toby opened the door to come in, he left it ajar, and a soft breeze swept through the church.

Rev. Brown had just begun to preach when a little yellowbird flew through the doorway. Everyone ignored the bird, but he flew from one stained glass window to another. He swooped over heads as he flew from the front of the church to the back and then to the front again.

Rev. Brown was preaching as if he had not noticed anything unusual, when suddenly the bird perched on Ms. Sherri's hat, then flew away again.

With not a hint of a smile on her face, Jackie wondered what she could do to help. She really wanted to laugh, but she remembered she was in God's House so she sat quietly and hoped the bird would not fly near her.

Soon he was back over Ms. Sherri's hat, moving in small circles, preparing to perch. Jackie realized why the bird had chosen that lady. She was wearing a hat all covered with pink flowers and green leaves. She glanced quickly at Mama, but she was wearing a snug white hat with a blue bow.

The preacher rolled his eyes and wiped his forehead with his handkerchief as the bird made his rounds from window to window and then past the preacher's head to Ms. Sherri's flowered hat.

Jackie prayed, "Dear God, please help the little bird find a way out." She opened her eyes just in time to see the little yellowbird fly out the door.

After the sermon, they all sang the closing hymn:
There is something on earth for the children to do
'Ere they go to that beautiful land
There's a pathway of love where the youngest may go
And employment for each little hand.
Though it may be but little, our Saviour once said,
If the little be given in love,
To the thirsty a drink, to the hungry some bread,
'Twill be surely rewarded above.
And the children can tell the sweet story of old,
Tell of Him by whom sin is forgiven,
And the Angels of God will rejoice if one soul
Should be led by the children to Heaven.

As they gathered around the dinner table, Mama said, "It was just God's mercy that nobody laughed or panicked during the service."

Jackie was thankful that Mama had not worn her hat with the yellow daisies.

"Mama, if it's okay with you, I'll cut the daisies off your hat, and put a white bow on it for you," Jackie said.

"Goodness no!" Mama replied. "You'll do no such thing! I like my hat just the way it is."

"Then I'll ask God to keep the little birds out of church when you wear it."

Daddy put down his fork and cleared his throat. "We'll go to Spotts this evening to visit your grandmother," he said. Shivers moved down Jackie's back as she remembered the waterlily pond and the frogs. "First we'll rest awhile. As always, you're not allowed to play on Sunday."

"If we're really good, can we go to Spotts beach and swim?" Judy asked.

"May we?" Mama corrected her.

"No!" Daddy said. "Tomorrow we'll go to the Seven-Mile Beach. We'll swim then. We might as well take advantage of the Easter Monday holiday."

Daddy wiped his mouth and excused himself. He picked up his pillow and headed for the printing shop to rest. Mama rocked in the hammock and Judy bounced a rubber ball.

"Stop that bouncing," Mama said.

So Judy, Jane, and Jackie took the ball with them out under the breadfruit tree. They played quietly and all went well until the ball crossed the fence and landed in Uncle Bill's yard.

"We'll lift you over the fence, Jackie, and you can go get it."

"No," Jackie said. "The two of you were acting like brats, throwing it to each other and leaving me out."

"Not so," Jane said.

"Don't worry," Judy told her. "We don't need her anyway. I'll get the ball."

Judy was checking out the fence, trying to figure out how to climb over it. She tried to pull and twist the heavy wires that formed the design on the fence, but she couldn't move them. She could find no place to put her feet to climb over.

Jane and Judy were whispering now, and Jackie couldn't hear what they said. While they whispered, they dug a hole under the fence.

Judy quit digging and began crawling beneath the fence. When she was halfway across, she became stuck, and Jane and Jackie tried to pull her out by the legs, but she didn't move.

"Go get Mama," Jane told Jackie, but instead, Jackie ran to the printing shop and called to Daddy from the doorway.

"Hurry, Daddy. Judy needs you," Jackie told him.

He looked stunned from sleep, and reached down for his shoes, but Jackie said, "No, Daddy. You must hurry." So he ran barefoot behind Jackie to the fence.

In a second, Daddy rested his hands on the top of that wire fence and glided over it to the other side. He began digging the dirt away from Judy's face with his hands.

"Run and get me the shovel," he said. "Hurry!"

When Jackie handed him the shovel, Daddy turned to Judy and said, "Don't panic. Daddy will get you out."

Jackie was wringing her hands and crying and praying. And all the while Daddy shoveled the sand deeper and deeper beside Judy. Jackie thought that Daddy was digging in the wrong place, but she trusted him, so she didn't say a word.

Finally, he told Judy, "Okay, Coo-Coo, Daddy is going to slide you sideways to the deeper hole that he just dug."

Jane stood pale and silent, and Jackie cried and worked with Daddy from the other side of the fence. Little by little, they slid Judy into the deep hole that Daddy had dug and she slipped free, all covered in dirt and sand.

Just then, Mama came out the back door.

"What's going on out here?" she asked.

When Daddy told her, she said, "Well, I guess God spared me this one."

They were all hugging Judy, and Daddy turned to her and said, "I don't know whether to hug you or spank you."

Then he said, "Come here," and he reached out and hugged her.

Jane was holding onto Mama's hand. Daddy hugged them and said, "Jane, I know you were praying!" Jackie wanted to say, *I was praying too,* but of course she didn't. Then he called to Jackie.

"Come here to me," Daddy said. He wiped the tears from her face with his handkerchief. "Thank you for working so hard with me," he said. Then he turned to Mama. "She's like you, Al-Al. She panics easily, but she's like me, too. She has that grit that helps to get her through rough times."

"I know," Mama told him. "I've always said she's more your child than mine."

5

THE FORBIDDEN MANGO

"Oh my," Mama said, "I hope she doesn't stop here."

Mama had said it more to herself in a low, muffled voice, but Jackie had heard the words as soon as she opened her eyes. She jumped out of her little bed and ran to Mama.

"What's wrong, Mama?" Jackie asked. "What is it? Who is that?"

Mama didn't answer her. She had fallen to her knees and was peering over the windowsill and through the opening in the curtains. A small figure of a woman swayed slowly along the side of the road, her dress skimming the street.

Mama reached out and grabbed Jackie by the sleeve of her nightgown. She pulled her behind a door and said, "I want her to go by."

"But why, Mama?"

"Shush," Mama whispered as she held her hand over Jackie's mouth.

Knock-knock. Knock-knock. A stick was hitting the porch rail. Jackie felt as Mama shivered. She stood stiff and still and said nothing.

Knock-knock. "Is anybody home?" a voice asked. "I come to speak to the lady of the house."

Mama slowly emerged, leaving Jackie still hiding behind the door.

"Oh, Ms. Dulcianna, how are you today?" Mama asked.

"Why, I'm doing just fine, thank you," the old woman said. "I decided to take a walk and come to visit you."

"Well, that's very sweet of you," Mama said.

Jackie inched her way to the window and hid and peeped through the curtains.

The old woman wore a long black dress with long sleeves and a white apron. *Swish-swish* went the broomweed in her hand as she fanned flies from around her face. She reached into her pocket and held something up toward Mama.

"I brought my prized mango to give you. It is one of the first to ripen from my Bombay mango tree."

"Well, don't you think you should have it?" Mama stuttered. "I wouldn't want to take it from you."

"No, my fair lady. It is yours. I brought it for you."

"Well, I'm very honoured, I'm sure," Mama said. "That is so kind of you. May I offer you something to drink? Some lemonade, perhaps?"

"Yes, thank you," the old woman said. Every few minutes she stuck out her tongue and rolled her eyes. She wiped her sweaty face with a handkerchief edged with lace as she sat on the swing on the porch.

Mama hurried to the kitchen, with Jackie one step behind her. She put the mango on a high shelf and poured a glass of lemonade. Then she turned to Jackie.

"Don't you even think of eating that. Don't touch it, don't smell it," Mama said.

Jackie would not touch it or eat it, but she had smelled it as Mama went by and it smelled so-o-o-o good.

Back at the window, Jackie saw Mama hand Ms. Dulcianna the lemonade, and she watched as she drank every drop. Then she stuck that tongue out again, fanned imaginary flies from her face and rolled her eyes.

"Oh, that was so good," she said. "Thank you, lady."

Daddy was by the printing shop window now, observing the anxious look on Mama's face. Soon he rounded the corner of the porch and stood on the steps.

"How are you today, Ms. Dulcianna?" Daddy asked.

"I'm just fine, Mr. Bodden. I came to bring your nice family a sweet, juicy Bombay mango. But I'm just about to be on my way. I must take the other mango to another friend down the road. She reached once more in her pocket and showed Daddy the mango.

Daddy helped her down the porch steps and wished her a nice day, and she went on her way.

Daddy and Mama came inside the house, and Mama's face was pale.

"She's bad luck," Mama said. "I wish she hadn't stopped here. Came to bring a mango! Of course we'll not eat it! I do believe people are right when they say she

was obeahed. Did you see how she sticks out her tongue and rolls her eyes?"

"Yeah," Jackie said. "Kind of like a lizard."

"No one asked for your opinion," Daddy said. "And that wasn't a very polite thing for you to say. You must learn to respect your elders."

"I'm sorry, Daddy," Jackie said. She said no more, but she listened.

"There's no such thing as obeah," Daddy told Mama. "Nor bad luck either. Well, I better get back to printing. I'm sure it's a perfectly good mango, but you do what you want with it."

Mama said not another word. She went to the kitchen, took the mango from the shelf and walked across the back yard to the fence. She stood there for a moment, then she slung the mango far into the bushes beyond the fence.

When she came back to the house she brushed past Jackie and washed her hands several times.

Jackie was like Mama. She still felt fear. Of what, she did not know. She got dressed and jumped the back fence to visit her friends, April and Kim. She told them all about the stranger on the porch.

The three girls stood beneath the guinep tree and picked bunches of guineps from the low branches. They sat on the ground cracking the green shell and sucking the pink, sour-sweet pulp from the marble-sized seeds. Every once in a while they stopped eating to discuss the stranger and the mango.

"Stop it, all of you," a voice said from the bushes nearby. "It's mine, I found it."

Jackie felt fear creep over her once more as she listened.

"I get to eat first, then I'll share with all of you," the voice from the bushes continued.

"Oh, no!" Jackie said. She ran toward the bushes and climbed between the barb wire fence.

"Who would have thought that this old mango tree would have such a delicious mango, and so early in the season? This tree, with it's wormy fruit, is finally bearing good mangoes." Jackie recognized Judy's voice.

"Stop it. Stop eating that mango!" Jackie yelled. She tore through the thick bushes and finally reached the girls. Judy's face was golden with mango juice and she had passed the mango on to Rita. Rita took several big bites before handing it to Kristy.

"That mango is bad for you," Jackie said. "Don't eat it." But Kristy sucked on the seed until it changed from golden to white. Then she buried it in the ground and wiped her mouth on her sleeve.

"Ms Dulcianna gave that mango to Mama and she was afraid of it, so she threw it away," Jackie told them.

Kristy bent forward and coughed a choking cough.

"Don't believe her," Rita said. She's just saying that because she didn't get any. Should have been here earlier. You could have gotten a bite."

Jackie had arrived too late to stop them from eating the forbidden mango, so she said no more.

At dinner Judy wasn't hungry and asked to be excused. Mama questioned what she might have eaten to kill her appetite.

"We were playing rounder and Rita hit the ball back in the bushes. We went to find it. Couldn't find the ball, but I found this big juicy mango way back under the old mango tree. Must have been the first one this season, because all the others are little and green."

Mama's voice trembled. "Oh, no!" was all she said.

"Anyway, I found it, so I ate most of it. It was almost orange inside. The sweetest mango I ever tasted. Shared it with Rita and Kristy, but Jackie found us too late to get some." Judy left the table and went to her room.

The fork fell from Mama's hand and her eyes studied Daddy's face.

"What shall we do?" Mama asked.

"Go for the doctor," Jackie said. "Quick."

"We'll do no such thing," Daddy said.

"Well, I'll keep her in the house the rest of the day, where I can observe her," Mama told him.

That night they rocked in the swing on the porch and relived that fearful day.

"Now I wish I could have tasted that mango," Jackie said.

"I wish you could have too," Daddy told her.

"Not me," Mama said. Then she turned to Daddy. "But I do believe that you're right. Perhaps there is no such thing as bad luck and obeah. I guess my fears kept us from tasting a perfectly good Bombay mango."

"Perhaps Ms. Dulcianna will bring you another one," Daddy said with a smile. But Mama shook her head. "No," she said. "On second thought, I think I'd rather not taste one."

6

A LOOK INSIDE THE CISTERN

"The water in the cistern is getting so low that we must begin boiling every drop that we drink," Mama told Baw Baw. "Let it boil hard for at least twenty minutes to kill the bacteria."

"Okay, Al-Al," Baw Baw said. "I been thinking that myself. There's no rain in sight, and us with rainy season still a couple of months away."

"Everybody's water is low now. I don't like to turn down anyone that might ask for a bucket of water, but we have to for their own safety."

"Sure do," Baw Baw said. "'Cause if we give them water and they don't boil it, they could get very sick with dysentery, and we don't want that sweeping the island."

Whatever dysentery is, it must be something bad, Jackie thought. She stuck a spoon in her oatmeal porridge. In the center of the table, in a bowl half-filled with water, sat the can of sweetened condensed milk. She reached for it and the milk slowly poured from the opening on one side of the can. She swirled it into her porridge with her spoon. Then she tasted it.

"Um-m-m," she said out loud to herself as she ate the first mouthful. "Just like pudding." She knew that she need never worry about ants getting into the can of milk as long as it was kept in a bowl of water. When she had finished eating she walked into the kitchen where Mama and Baw Baw still discussed the water crisis.

"I don't like boiled water, Mama. It tastes really bad," Jackie said.

"Well it's pretty good when Baw Baw cools it and pours it into the clay cooler on the shelf. That keeps it nice and fresh."

"I still don't like it, Mama!"

"Well, you have no choice. Drink it from the little calabash that Washerwoman gave you. She says water tastes better from a calabash."

"But couldn't I just drink water at some of my friends' houses instead?"

"No!" Mama said. "No! Everybody's cistern is low now, and I don't want you drinking any water that is not boiled."

Baw Baw pulled the largest pot from the cupboard. "Well, I might as well begin right now." She took it to the cistern and placed it on the cement step beside the cistern window. She pulled a key from her pocket and unlocked the padlock that kept the cistern window secure at all times.

Jackie ran outside and inched her way beside Baw Baw as she took the dipper from the nail just inside the cistern window.

"You too close to me," Baw Baw said. "You not s'posed to be no way near the cistern when it's open."

"But I want to see in it, Baw Baw. Please let me see."

"You might as well let her take a look," Mama called from the kitchen window. "Maybe then she'll understand what we're warning her about."

Baw Baw stepped aside so as not to block the view. She twisted the hem of Jackie's dress around her hand and held tightly to it as Jackie peered down. Then she loosened the rope, slowly lowering the dipper. Down, down, down it went.

Finally there was a *splish-splash* below as it reached the water. Jackie saw that the cistern, with its walls reaching deep down below the level of the ground, was almost empty. The open window cast a dim light all the way down.

"Oh-o-o," Jackie said. "So-o-o scary." Baw Baw jerked her arm from side to side and the dipper filled with water and sank the short distance to the bottom. She released Jackie's skirt and pushed her away from the window.

There was a scratching and splashing sound as the dipper hit the sides of the cistern while she pulled it up. Then she poured the water in the pot.

"You know, Baw Baw, I've tried to look through the window on the other side many times, but I can't see through it."

"No, because the holes that they punched in the heavy tin covering that window are too small to see through. Not even a mosquito can get through those tiny holes."

"Then what good is the window, if it can't open and you can't see through it?" Jackie asked.

"'Cause that window over there is for ventilation. Everything needs air. Now, don't ask anymore questions. Run and play."

Baw Baw lowered the dipper and splashed it around in the water again. When it was full she pulled it up and poured it into the pot on the step. She twirled the rope around and around in circles and returned the dipper to its place on the nail inside the cistern. Then she shut and padlocked the door.

The water looked just fine to Jackie, nice and clear, but of course she remembered learning in school that you could not always see germs.

Sitting in its place on a back burner of the wood-burning stove, the pot would be left to slowly simmer and then boil.

Jackie looked toward the back corner of the yard. Perhaps she should jump the fence and see if April wanted to play. When she had taken only a few steps toward it, she heard a noise.

Daddy was leaning his bicycle against a post. She turned and followed him as he almost ran toward the house.

"What are you doing home so early from work?" Mama asked.

"I'm going to take the car and pick up Konrad, if he's home. Rain is coming. Lots of it! Probably this weekend. I'll see if he can clean the cistern today, before the rains hit."

"I hope you're right" Mama said. "But the sky is blue. Really blue!"

He turned and hurried away, but Jackie caught up with him.

"Did you hear that at the Wireless Station, Daddy?"

"Yes, Coo-Coo. The weather bureau report! Now run along and play."

Jackie stood there for a moment after she had waved to Daddy. *Why did everybody want her to run along and play when they were busy? But when she wanted to run and play they were always calling her back home?*

7

THE EMPTY CISTERN

Jackie drew a hopscotch square behind the kitchen and hopped and skipped all by herself as she waited for Daddy to return.

She heard a screeching sound and looked up. Straddling the carport a short distance from her was Daddy's car. The doors opened and Daddy and Mr. Konrad and Mr. Konrad's son, Skippy, got out.

Immediately, Mr. Konrad washed the big drum at the side of the cistern and drained it. He loosed the rope from the dipper and tied it to a big bucket. He was bailing the water out and pouring it into the drum to save it. He walked toward the printing shop and opened the back door. The clanking of the printing press thundered through the door.

"I've bailed about all I can bail from here," Mr. Konrad yelled above the noise.

Daddy shut down the press and stepped out the back door and into the yard. "That's good, Konrad," He said. "It's moving fast."

Daddy showed him where the ladder was stored in the crawl space beneath the house and Mr. Konrad pulled it out and washed it down. Then he lowered it into the cistern. He took off his shoes and washed his feet.

"Skippy, this is where I need your help. I'm going down into the cistern. After I've scrubbed down the walls I will scoop out the water that's still down there and I'll need you to pull the dipper up."

"I understand, Papa," Skippy said. "I'll do that."

Mr. Konrad loosed the rope from the bucket and tied the small dipper back on the rope. Then he took the dipper down the ladder with him.

For a while nothing seemed to be happening, except the scratching sound that floated up from the cistern. Skippy sat on the cistern step and aimed his slingshot at Daddy's garden.

Jackie threw a piece of broken glass from one part of the hopscotch to another and she hopped and listened and watched.

Old Smokey, the cat, lay nearby, one front leg covering his eyes. Jumping at the slightest noise, he would open one eye and peep at Jackie. Occasionally Mama looked out the window at the blue sky and shook her head.

"I'm ready for you to pull up the dipper, Skippy," Mr. Konrad called from deep down in the cistern. "But don't throw the water into the drum."

"Why not, Papa?"

"'Cause the silt from the bottom of the cistern is stirred up and mixed into the water. It's muddy. It would ruin the clear water in the drum."

"I understand, Papa," Skippy said. "I'll throw it on the garden."

"Good idea. That way it won't be wasted," Mr. Konrad said.

Skippy pulled up dipper after dipper full of the murky water. He threw it all in Daddy's garden. The sand and dust rolled down slope with the water. Still he threw more on it. Splish-splash went the water.

"You're pouring too much water on the garden," Jackie told him.

"No. It'll. . . it'll do it good," he told her.

"I'll stop now," the call came from down deep in the cistern. "It's almost empty."

Jackie wanted to see what an empty cistern looked like, so she inched her way over to the open window and peeped down in it. It was totally empty except for a basin in the middle of the cistern floor.

She could see that all sides sloped toward it, and the last tiny bit of water had collected in the basin. Mr. Konrad scooped it up with a calabash and poured it into the dipper and the cistern was empty. He held the dipper in his hand and walked toward the ladder. Then he carefully began climbing the ladder with the last dipper of water in his hand. Jackie backed away and went toward her hopscotch.

Mr. Konrad climbed out and poured the last of the water on the ground. Then he rinsed the dipper, hung it inside the cistern and pulled the ladder up, returning it to where Daddy kept it.

Daddy thanked him and paid him. He asked if he could come back the following day to clean the gutters. Mr. Konrad said he would be there bright and early. Then he and Skippy left for home.

That evening at supper, Daddy looked across the table at Mama, "I couldn't believe my eyes when I went out to work in the garden this evening," he said. "Skippy washed it all away. Sand gone from the roots. Plants leaning or flat on the ground. I found one pepper plant almost down to the fence."

"Oh, no," Mama said. Then they both began to laugh and Daddy said, "Well, you win some and lose some, and that's the way life goes."

8

THE INVISIBLE LOBSTER

Tarla came by and invited Jackie to go swimming in Papa's bay across the street.

"Please, Mama, may I go?" Jackie asked.

"I had planned on you helping me around the house today," Mama told her. "The skirts to your school uniforms all need lengthening, and I thought you could take care of your little brother while I sew."

"I could take John swimming with us!"

"You'll do no such thing!" Mama told her. "Even though he can swim, he's still too young to go near the water unless your father or myself is there."

"Please, Mama. We only have a few more days of spring vacation!"

"Your whole life is a vacation," Jackie heard Baw Baw mumble from the kitchen.

"Well," Mama said. "I guess you can go. It's not often that Tarla comes to go swimming, and you'll be just across the street."

Jackie changed to her bathing suit and grabbed an inflated inner tube. The two girls ran toward the bay.

"Throw the tube in and let's jump on it," Tarla said.

Tarla jumped first and the tube sank and rose and dumped her out of it.

"My turn," Jackie yelled. She waved her arm impatiently as Tarla lingered beneath her. "Move away so I don't jump on you."

She jumped and tumbled and rolled in the water. Later as they rocked on the piece of rope that had been tied across the narrow bay, Jackie saw the strange creature move beneath the edge of the big rock.

"What's that?" she yelled as she splashed her feet against the water below the rope, in an effort to rock faster. She pointed to the huge rock all covered with brown and green moss.

"What are you talking about?" Tarla asked. "I don't see anything." Jackie shook the rope and Tarla fell off into the water. Then Jackie fell. Tarla was peering at the big rock and sticking her foot near it.

"Stop it," Jackie told her. "I saw a crab or something crawl under that rock." She went out of the water and found a stick beneath a popnut tree and she jumped back in. She poked the stick beneath the rock and felt something move.

"Just leave it alone," Tarla said. "I don't even want to know what it is."

"Course, you do!" Jackie told her. "It might be your only chance to see an octopus!"

Jackie curved the stick around beneath the rock and pulled the creature out.

"A lobster," she yelled as it came into full view, then crawled back beneath the rock. In her haste to get away from it her foot slipped and hit something.

"Ouch!" Jackie cried. "It bit me. Oh, no, I'm allergic to lobsters and it bit me."

"Lobsters don't bite, silly. They pinch. Should've left it alone," Tarla said, but she helped Jackie to shore. When finally they were out of the water, they realized that Jackie had stepped on a sea urchin and her foot was crammed with the black bristles.

A couple of those prongs had broken beyond the skin of her heel and they wiggled as if they were still alive on the sea urchin. Tarla tried to pull them out but they broke off close to the skin. Tears rolled down Jackie's face, but she did not cry.

"Goodness," Mama said, when finally they had crossed the street for home. "I don't know that I've ever seen so many sea eggs in one foot. What were you doing?"

"I saw a big lobster, Mama. The biggest one I've ever seen. He was beneath that old rock all covered with moss."

"Sure you saw a lobster," Tarla said. "An invisible one!"

"I did too see one," Jackie said. "And Mama, I'm afraid I might have killed him. I held him down with a big stick. Then I felt as if he broke free and I never saw him again."

"He's probably fine," Mama said. "Now, get under the pump and get your bath. Afterwards we'll put something on that foot."

"Why are you getting a bath under the outside pump?" Tarla asked.

"Because there's no water in the cistern. Anyway, it's fun taking turns pumping the well water."

First Jackie pumped the hand pump back and forth. The water rolled out and she handed Tarla the soap. Then Tarla pumped so hard that the water gushed out and almost took Jackie's breath away.

"We won't have to wash our bathing suits because they're getting washed under the pump," Tarla said.

"Right," Jackie agreed, "but soap doesn't lather good in brackish water."

Just then Baw Baw stuck her head out of the door. "Trying to pump the well dry?" she asked.

They heard voices in the distance and they ducked inside the kitchen door.

"Don't bring ya'all's sandy feet in this kitchen," Baw Baw said. "I just scrubbed the floor."

Tarla pulled her dress over her bathing suit and headed for home. Jackie rinsed her feet off and went inside the house to get dressed. Mama heated menthol salve and rubbed it on her foot. When she had slipped a sock over it, she hopped outside once more and sat beneath the big breadfruit tree.

Mr. Konrad stood outside Daddy's door. "Well, I didn't get here bright and early, but I got here bright," he said.

Jackie could tell by the stern look on Daddy's face that he didn't think it was funny.

"Here is the new screen to cover the end of the gutter inside the cistern," Daddy told him. "Be very careful when you take the old screen off. Hold a bucket beneath it so that none of the trash from the old screen falls into the cistern."

"Yes, sir. I'll do that," Mr. Konrad said. "In fact, I'll do that first."

"I'll work with you until that is done," Daddy said. He stepped down from the printing shop and walked toward the cistern. When he came to the joint in the rounded gutter, he pulled it apart. Jackie saw that this left a shorter piece of gutter protruding into the cistern through the roof.

Mr. Konrad did just as Daddy had told him to do. He opened the cistern window and removed the screen and trash, and let them fall into the bucket he held beneath it. Then he called to Daddy to jerk the piece of gutter out of the roof of the cistern.

"Well, the most important part is done, and the cistern is still clean," Daddy said. He left to go back to his printing.

Mr. Konrad stuck his hand in the rounded gutter and pulled out leaves and trash. He took it over to the pump and pumped well water through it until the water poured clean.

Mr. Konrad's son, Skippy, had come back again to help his Dad. He seemed anxious to get his work over with.

He got the ladder and leaned it against the far end of the house. Climbing halfway up, he stuck his hand in the open gutter that was attached along the edge of the roof.

"Lots of leaves and breadfruit pods up here, Papa," he said, "and grime."

"Well, clean it out good, son. That's why I brought you along." And all the while, Mr. Konrad continued to work, cleaning out portions of the round gutter.

It seemed to Jackie that they were tearing the gutters all apart, and after what Skippy had done to Daddy's garden the day before, she felt a bit anxious.

"I got all the leaves out, Papa," he said. "Can I go fish awhile off the shore?"

"I guess so son. Run along." Skippy picked up his fishing line and left.

Mr. Konrad cleaned and washed and wiped the gutters and finally he was ready to put them back together again.

Daddy left his printing and came once more to help. "This part is a two-man job," he said. They worked together until the rounded gutters had been hooked back up to the joints that held them together. When the end piece was fitted back through the roof of the cistern, Daddy washed off the old piece of screen and used it for a pattern to cut the new screen. He opened the cistern and fitted the screen over the gutter that protruded inside the cistern. Then he wired the screen tightly to the gutter.

"Well, Konrad, it can rain now. We're ready for it." Daddy said.

"Yes sir, we're ready."

"I'll not hook the cistern gutter up to the rest until the first heavy rains wash the roof clean."

Mama came outside and smiled that the work had gone so well.

Daddy paid Mr. Konrad and went back to work, and Mr. Konrad called to Skippy. A few minutes later, Skippy came through the gate.

"Look what I caught," he said, and he held up a lobster. "Didn't get no fish. Just this. Saw it in the bay and jumped in after it."

"Good for us," his Papa told him. "You caught our dinner."

"But look, Papa, it only has one claw."

Mama looked across at Jackie and nodded her head and Jackie winked and smiled.

9

A PIRATE'S TREASURE

"Who would have thought we would be facing a Nor'wester so late in the season?" Baw Baw asked. "And us with no drinking water in the cistern."

"The barrel of water will hold us over a few more days, if we're careful," Mama told her. "But you're right, that breeze is shifting to the Northwest."

Jackie ran to the porch to feel the cool Nor'wester breeze. Boats were headed out of the harbour and around the southernmost part of the Island.

Far up the road, she could see Captain Bodden and his son, Troy, working in their boat. Jackie knew that they were preparing to hoist the boat up high on stilts where the seas could not reach it. She had seen them pull those ropes and hoist it many times.

She ran inside to tell Mama the news.

"All the boats are headed for Spotts," Jackie told her.

"Yes," Mama said. "They'll be safe up there."

"And Daddy sent Todd down on his bicycle to tell you that he won't be home for dinner."

Mama turned pale and looked at Baw Baw. "Must be a bad one, if he can't leave the Wireless Station to come home for the noon meal. We'll use the chicken and sea pie that was left over from yesterday, and add potato salad and baked plantain and rice."

"Goodness," Baw Baw said, "and me with red beans already cooking in this big pot of coconut milk. How do you expect me to get all this done?"

"I'll work with you," Mama said. "You run along, Jackie, and reserve the taxi for twelve noon."

"Okay, Mama," Jackie said, but she stopped and joined a game of rounder in the street.

"Throw the ball to second base," Kristy yelled to Jackie. "If you want to be on our team, you'll have to play like you want to win."

Jackie's heart just wasn't in the game, so she went back home. Mama was busy in the kitchen, rinsing her best plate and bowl and pulling her silver tray out of the china cabinet.

"You get so flustered, A1-A1," Baw Baw said. "You're okay for big happenings, but you fall apart fixing Tatti's food."

"I guess you're right," Mama said. "We didn't need all this extra work today, though."

Jackie was sorry that she had told Mama such a thing! She would tell her differently in just a little while. She went back on the porch to watch the boats. Lindy called and asked if she would like to spend the day with her. They could dig for pirates' treasures, Lindy said.

Jackie ran back to the kitchen for Mama's permission.

"Yes," Mama told her. "You'll just be next door."

"Thank goodness," Baw Baw said. "She needed something to keep her busy!"

Jackie and Lindy crossed the street with hand shovels and garden tools, and headed for the big rock on the bay across from Lindy's house.

The sea was surging now and the waves hit the shore, sprinkling salt spray over the two girls. They giggled and dug beneath the huge rock and told pirate stories.

"Take a look at this," Lindy said. Sitting atop a shovelful of dirt was a piece of green glass, all cloudy-looking and smooth on the edges.

"That's got to mean something," Jackie said. "We'll keep it as our first treasure."

"It means something, all right. It means it was in the water a long time before it ended up under the rock."

"Well, that's okay," Jackie told her. "I'll keep it anyway." Now, they began to dig furiously.

"What is this?" Jackie asked. "Oh, my goodness. A bone. I'll not touch it."

"Me neither," Lindy said, so Jackie put that shovelful of dirt with the bone beside the green glass.

"You know, the story goes that they always buried someone on top of their treasure to guard the gold."

"Yeah," Lindy agreed. "Someone with a hatchet in his hand."

Something rattled each time the shovel touched it. *Perhaps it was a pirate's treasure chest!* So they dug and they dug with the shovel, too afraid to stick a hand under the rock and pull it out. Dirt hit Jackie in the eye, causing it to sting, but she kept on digging.

Looking down at the rusty tin can in the dirt, she could barely read the words, *Talcum Powder*. She shook it but nothing escaped the tiny holes on the top. Still, the tin can rattled. Lindy perched it on the big rock and hit it with a smaller one. The top flew off, spilling black, rusty coins over the ground.

"We found it," Jackie yelled. "The pirate's treasure. Let's clean these coins with a breadfruit leaf and some wet sand and ashes." So, they scrubbed and scrubbed the coins like they had seen Washerwoman scrub the bottoms of the cooking pots when she helped with washing dishes.

"Now, we're ready for Daddy to tell us what they're worth."

The girls ran toward the fence just in time to see Daddy's car creep along, chug-a-lugging as he turned into the carport.

"Oh no!" Jackie said. "I forgot to tell Mama something!"

"Well, let it go," Lindy told her. "Let's see what your dad thinks of these coins."

Daddy held a few in his hand and peered down at them. "Uh-huh," Daddy said as he turned them over to read the writing.

"So?" Jackie asked impatiently.

"They're just old coins. Someone probably collected them years ago -- perhaps even buried them."

"But what are they worth, Daddy? Will we be rich?"

"I hardly think so, but you can keep them anyway."

"And the bone?" Lindy asked.

"Just a chicken bone," Daddy told her.

So Jackie and Lindy sat by the fence and shared their treasure.

Mama hurried toward Daddy. "Why are you home so early?" She asked.

"Early?" Daddy questioned. "It's my regular time."

"Well, I have your dinner all ready and the taxi was to be here shortly to take it to the Wireless Station."

Daddy looked puzzled. Jackie stopped sharing the money. Mama's face was covered with red splotches. She slipped a soft shoe from one foot.

"Jacqueline, come home right now," she said through clenched teeth.

"I can't," Jackie said. "I'm spending the day with Lindy. Remember?"

"Well, you're not anymore," Mama said.

Tears rolled down Jackie's face. "I meant to tell you, Mama, but then I started digging for treasure and I forgot, but I never asked the taxi driver to come by."

Daddy had a crooked smile on his face and Jackie saw his gold tooth shine in the sun just before he turned his face so Mama couldn't see him smile.

"Wait a minute," Daddy said. He turned to Mama. "I'll bet you forgot that it's April Fools Day. Let her go! We pulled those pranks on our parents many times, didn't we?"

Mama's face softened and she slipped her shoe back on.

Lindy's mother was calling the girls to eat their noon meal. They ate red beans and flour dumplings cooked in coconut milk and rice, and potato salad.

"These are the best beans and rice I've ever tasted," Jackie said as she finished and excused herself from the table. "I wish Baw Baw could cook them good like you."

Lindy's mother smiled but said nothing. That afternoon Jackie went home, taking with her half of the coins.

Salt spray drifted across the street now and settled on everything in its path. Rain fell in sheets, and Jackie and her sisters played in the rain water that spouted from the unhitched gutter.

Finally, Mama called them inside to get dressed. Later, around the supper table, Daddy thanked God for the food and the rain.

"If the waves would die down, you could hook up the gutters and the cistern would be full in no time," Mama said.

"It'll probably slow up by tomorrow," Daddy told her. "Then I'll have to wait for the rain to wash the salt spray from the roof, so it doesn't ruin the water. But according to the weather report, it should rain for a few days yet."

Jackie scooped up some potato salad and beans and dumplings and put them on her plate.

"Why are you wearing sunglasses, Jackie?" Jane asked.

"My eye hurts, 'cause a pirate or something slung dirt in it."

"Oh?" Jane smiled. "A pirate, eh?"

Jackie's fork was chasing a dumpling round and round in her plate. She wiped the tears from her sore eye on her sleeve. From the corner of her eye, she could see Daddy smiling.

"Seems I ate this for dinner today," Daddy said.

"You did," Mama told him. "There was so much food cooked this morning that I told Baw Baw not to try and come back out to prepare supper. I even handed Lindy's mother a big bowl of the beans and dumplings over the fence. That kept her from having to cook today."

"Lindy's mother?" Jackie asked. "Beans and dumplings? Baw Baw's?"

"What's wrong with you?" Judy asked.

"Nothing!" Jackie said.

10

THE SECONDHAND COFFIN

"Cut the paper straight," Judy told Jackie. "Try to do a better job."

"Well, the crepe paper is folded too thick and the scissors are hurting my finger," Jackie told her.

"Then pass it to me. I'll get it done faster. We must hurry. The morning is slipping by."

Jackie handed Judy the scissors. She laid the strips that she had cut in the wheelbarrow that Daddy kept in the crawl space beneath the store.

"Why can't we go under the big sea grape tree and cut them?" Jackie asked. "It's hot under here".

"'Cause the breeze would scatter the paper and nosey passersby would ask questions," Judy told her. "Now get on with your work. Pin these safety pins, one on each strip of the paper."

Jackie did as she was told. Soon the sisters crawled out, taking their morning's work with them.

"Now, we'll go in the store and try to pin paper tails on the customers."

"But won't we get in trouble?" Jackie asked.

"Not if we're careful. I'll show you how."

Judy kept the paper in a roll and when a customer went up to the counter, she walked behind her.

"Oh, Ms. Dova, you have a button that is open. I'll button it for you," she said. Then she pinned the paper tail on Ms. Dova and she left the store, the pink paper strip trailing behind her. It all looked so easy, Jackie thought.

"You're next," Judy said to Jackie. Ms. Iris, the clerk, pretended not to have seen as she waited on customers.

"Here comes Aunt Tillie," Judy said.

Aunt Tillie went up to the counter and asked to buy a pound of brown sugar and a piece of cheese.

"Your apron is coming loose," Jackie told her. "Do you want me to tie it?"

"Yes, child," Aunt Tillie said and with trembling fingers, Jackie pinned the paper tail to her apron string.

Unrolling as Aunt Tillie walked away, the breeze rippled yards and yards of pink crepe paper behind her. Jackie giggled and Judy prepared for the next customer.

Then Aunt Tillie stepped back in the store door. Her face was red and she could hardly speak. She wanted to see Daddy, but he was at work at the Wireless Station. She crossed the street to the house. A short pink tail still rippled behind her, the rest had been caught in a fence and left behind. She spoke with Mama on the porch.

"Don't worry, Aunt Tillie, I'll take care of it," Jackie heard Mama say.

Aunt Tillie left and Mama called her girls home.

"Which of you pinned that tail on Aunt Tillie?" Mama asked.

"I did," Jackie said. "But it was all in fun, since today is Tail Day."

"I know it's Tail Day," Mama said. "It seems everybody I've seen this morning has had a paper or cloth tail flying behind them. But Aunt Tillie didn't think it was funny, and neither do I. You'll stay inside the rest of the day. Both of you! You've had your fun for the day."

Judy went to her room, but Jackie threw her pillow on the floor beside the back bedroom door. As she lay there, a gentle breeze fanned her face. She watched as a woodpecker pecked in the pear tree, the feathers on his head standing tall as he searched for food.

Ground doves covered the sandyard and ate the chicken feed that Daddy had thrown out for the chicks. Then they went to the water trough and bathed in the chickens' water.

Jackie fell asleep. When she awoke it was evening. Jane was getting friends together for a game of hide-and-go-seek.

Mama said she hoped that Jackie and Judy had learned their lesson for the day, so now they could go out and play with the others.

Rita covered her eyes and counted to twenty. All went in search of a hiding place. Jackie tagged along with Jane and Missy. They watched as Matt hid inside Washerwoman's washtub as it leaned against a tree. Kristy stood beside an over-turned canoe that was being repaired under an almond tree.

Then they stumbled by a shed that was built high in the air on tall stilts.

"Let's hide in the shed," Jane said. "They'll never find us there."

"No, it's too dark up there," Jackie said. "Frogs might be in it."

Missy convinced her that it was a safe place to hide, so one by one they climbed the ladder.

"One, two, three," Rita yelled. "Coming ready or not." The familiar words echoed through the shed and the girls giggled quietly as they thought of their hiding place.

They inched their way along, inside the dark shed, and soon they tripped over something. Thinking it only a piece of board, they stepped over it and sat on the edge. Their feet dangled along the side of the board and Jackie giggled, "They'll never find us in here."

"I found you, Judy," Rita's voice came from a distance. "Now you can help me find the others."

"Let's get 'em," Judy said.

"Oh, no," Kristy said as Rita pulled her from the overturned canoe. Now there were three seekers.

"We found you, Matt," a voice said. "Come on down from the tree limb, Brian. We see you."

"Now, let's see," Judy said. "Only Jane, Missy and Jackie left to find."

The three girls snickered, wondering why the others had not looked in the shed.

"The only place left to look is the shed," they heard Brian say. "And I'm not going in there because a coffin is inside the shed."

"Don't believe them," Missy said. "They're only trying to scare us into coming down."

Jackie chewed her bubble gum and blew bubbles and whispered, "I wonder who they think they're scaring?"

"You better come down. We know you're up there, but we're not coming up because Mr. Gordie's coffin is in there," Brian yelled.

Mr. Gordie was very sick and Jackie began to wonder if maybe he had bought himself a coffin and put it in the shed.

"You know, maybe they're right," Jane whispered. "Maybe we should go down."

"I'm no fraidycat," Missy told her. "I'm staying right here until they come and get me."

"Me too, I'm no fraidycat either," Jackie's voice trembled as she uncurled her toes. For a while all was quiet, and then there was a loud thud inside the shed.

"We threw up a flashlight," Rita said. "Turn it on and take a look for yourself."

Jackie's hand fumbled on the floor in search of the flashlight.

"Weeeeee, a coffin," she cried, "And we're sitting inside of it."

Missy and Jane screamed and hurried down the ladder with the flashlight. The others laughed and laughed and ran in different directions.

Jackie bruised her knee trying to jump out of the coffin. Finally she reached the ladder and jumped down from the shed. Sitting on the ground, groaning with pain from her aching knee and stone-bruised heels, she realized that they had all gone and left her. Like Little Br'er Rabbit in her storybook, she hopped toward home.

Shortly before Jackie reached her gate she heard Missy tell Jane, "It's such a shame! Now poor old Mr. Gordie will have to be buried in a secondhand coffin."

11

IF ONLY DUPPIES COULD PINCH

Jackie heard people laughing out on the road in front of the house. She ran to the porch just in time to see Mr. Phil and Mr. Harley coming down the road. Each man held a paint can in one hand and an unlit lantern in the other.

It was 7:00 a.m. and Daddy had crossed the street to open the store. He stopped to watch the two brothers as they came nearer.

Phil swayed from one side of the road to the other, slapped his brother on the back, and laughed, Ha-ha-ha. Harley put his paint can on the side of the road, sat on it, and laughed, He-he-he-he.

Daddy spread his handkerchief on the store step and sat on it. He began laughing and took his pipe out of his mouth. Jackie moved to the swing. She covered her mouth and snickered, even though she did not yet know why she was laughing.

Finally, the two men staggered the short distance to the store. They sat beside Daddy on the steps and began telling him what was so funny.

"We left home long before daylight," Phil told Daddy. "Going to catch hermit crabs, or soldiers as we call them. Needed them for fish bait. Well, we looked in our mother's old yard, and under leaves and among rocks. Not a soldier was in sight."

"That's strange," Daddy said. "Usually they're all over the place, moving in a line, like marching soldiers."

Jackie shuddered as she remembered that once she had been bitten by a soldier. She could still feel the weight of that small land crab with his big borrowed shell on his back. She looked down at the scar on her finger that reminded her it really did happen.

"Well, not last night," Phil said. "No lines. No soldiers.

"Harley made up a soldier song. Sing it for him, Harley." Phil pulled his harmonica from his pocket. He rocked his head back and forth as he played it and Harley sang:

Dog war in grandma's yard
Don't go near
Dog war in grandma's yard
No soldiers there.

"See, what did I tell you? He's good with those songs, ain't he?"

"Yes, he is," Daddy said.

"Anyway, getting back to my story," Mr. Phil said. "We arrived at the almond trees between here and the churchyard. Almonds were all over the ground, but not a soldier feeding on them.

" 'You see any soldiers yet?' Harley asked me.

"'Not many, one or two,' I told him.

"'Let's go inside the churchyard, Phil. We always find soldiers in there.'

"'Okay,' I said. 'Let's go.'

"We walked on, stopping every once in a while to listen to the parrots jabbering high in the almond trees. Finally, we were there. We moved among the tombs where long ago they buried bodies in the churchyard. Among them we saw the unused tombs that had been abandoned when the new cemetery was made.

"Then we moved in different directions, holding our lanterns so low that they barely skimmed the ground. Plop, plop went my can as I threw two soldiers in it. Then I heard a faint *click, click, click* in the distance as three crab shells hit the bottom of Harley's can.

"We had wandered far apart, but I continued finding soldiers. I peeped inside one of the tiny tent-looking cement tombs. It was so c-r-e-e-p-y. I saw an opening on the opposite end.

"Sprawled across the whole inside of the tomb a family of soldier crabs marched. Sat my lantern down on the ground outside, then crawled inside with my paint can. Heard nothing beyond the scratching of the soldiers inside the can.

"It was still very dark. My hands fumbled around on the wall and ground, picking up first one soldier and then another. Now, my can was almost full and I was happy!

"Suddenly, my hand touched something warm. I jumped and bumped my head on the roof of the tomb. I couldn't have felt what I thought I did! A hand. Or was it a hand?

"I told myself 'I'll touch it again,' then, 'No, I'll not touch it.' Then, 'Yes, I will!'

"Finally, I inched my hand closer and touched it. It was then that I felt fingers. And just to be sure it was a hand, I pinched it.

"I was so scared that I crawled out of the tomb and ran down the road as fast as my legs would go. Then I saw Harley sitting by the side of the road, all pale and tired.

"'What you doing, Harley?' I asked, 'Sitting here looking like . . . like a dog panting for breath?'

"'I would tell you, but you . . . you wouldn't believe me,' Harley stammered.

"'After what just happened to me, I'll believe anything,' I told him. 'Anything.'

"'Well,' Harley told me, 'I wandered by an open tomb and poked my head inside. A whole family of soldiers had made their home there, so I began filling my paint can. Then a duppy pinched me.'

"I threw my head back and I laughed, *ha, ha, ha*. 'Did you say a duppy pinched you?'

'I told you that you wouldn't believe me,' Harley said. 'But it really happened. A duppy pinched my hand.'

"I put my arm around his shoulder and said, 'I've got good news for you, old boy. I was the duppy that pinched your hand, and I'm sure glad that you were the duppy that I pinched. We had both forgotten that each tomb had a front entrance and a back one.'

"We had to go back to the churchyard to get our lanterns and paint cans. When we arrived there, I said, 'You go first, Harley.'

"'Not me,' Harley said. 'I'm not going back in there. You go get the lanterns and paint cans. I'll wait right here.'

"Finally, we walked side by side into the churchyard, and over beside the tomb. As we bent down to pick up our lanterns, we saw them! The overturned paint cans. All the soldiers had escaped.

"The sun was peeking over the breadfruit trees by then, so we decided to go home. And here we are!"

"And we won't go fishing today," Harley added.

Daddy couldn't stop laughing. He wiped the tears of laughter from his face.

"Well, I know one thing for sure," Daddy told them. "There are happy soldiers running free in the churchyard today."

12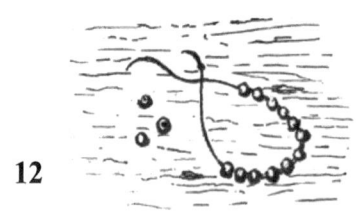

ISLAND DOCTOR

Jackie coughed and wheezed and coughed again. Her sides ached and her chest hurt and it was hard to breathe. Mama said sick little girls belonged in bed.

Baw Baw came into the room and stood beside her. "Poor you," she said. "You got the wheezing?" Then she touched Jackie's forehead to see if she had a fever. In her other hand she held a ripe sweetsop. "The sweetsop you been watching on the tree by the garage was ripe today. The little birds fought me for it, but I shooed them away and picked it for you."

"Oh, thank you, Baw Baw." Jackie said. The pegs of the sweetsop had burst open and Jackie could see the white juice inside. She tasted it and it was so sweet that she kept on eating until there was nothing left but a handful of black seeds and the green bumpy skin.

"See, your old Baw Baw knows what you like," she said. "Now lean back on those pillows and get a nap." But Jackie couldn't sleep. It was just too hard to breathe.

She watched as Mama put a spoon of dry mustard and four spoons of flour in a bowl. She poured warm water in the bowl and stirred it around until it looked like gold paste. Then she smeared it on a piece of flannel and folded a second piece over the top of it. She lit the kerosene lamp and held it above the lamp chimney until it was warm to touch. Then she blew out the light.

"Turn over," she said to Jackie. "Let me get this mustard plaster on your back." Mama put a dry washcloth over the plaster to keep it from staining Jackie's pajamas. Soon it began to feel hot, and Mama moved it to the other side of her back for a while, then between her shoulders, then in the middle of her back. Still Jackie coughed.

That afternoon she fell asleep. When she awoke, Mama was still sitting beside her. Because the mustard plaster had stayed too long on that spot on her back, she had a burned mark and blisters. Mama sprinkled powder on it to soothe it.

Daddy came in from the printing shop. He sat on the edge of the bed, his unlit pipe in his shirt pocket.

"Sing me the wounded soldier song, Daddy," Jackie said.

Daddy smiled and sang:

Oh, I'm just a wounded soldier
Returning from the war
With a cut across my forehead
And a half a dozen more.
My eyes are dim, I cannot see
And my head is hanging low,
I got one shoe on the wrong foot,
And I lost one big toe.

Daddy's song always made her feel a bit better and he always sang it when she was sick.

"I think you should go and get the doctor," Mama said.

"Yes, you're probably right," Daddy told her. "I know she's sick when she doesn't want to go outside and play".

"I like the doctor," Jackie said. "He laughs *HO HO HO,* like Santa Claus, and he puts his hand up by his ear when I answer his questions".

"Well, that's because he was in the war," Daddy told her. "The noise of battle damaged his ears and left him almost deaf."

"But he has nice eyes," Jackie said, "blue and soft, like my cat's eyes."

"Are you talking about Old Smokey?" Daddy asked. "You think Old Smokey has nice eyes?" Daddy took his unlit pipe from his pocket and stuck it in his mouth. It whistled as he sucked air through it. "Well, I must leave to go and pick up the doctor and bring him back. "Be a good girl, Coo-Coo. Try to get some rest."

After he left, Washerwoman came to visit Jackie.

"My-oh-my," Washerwoman said. "You got the phthisic?" Jackie nodded.

"Well, my dear, hurry and get better so you can sit under the breadfruit tree and help Washerwoman sing. It's all the swimming you do gives you the phthisic. Too much sun. Hold out your hand. I brought you something."

Jackie held out her hand and Washerwoman poured beads in it.

"Oh, thank you!" Jackie exclaimed. "Thank you."

Washerwoman's eyes twinkled and she said, "Okay, I'll be back to see you tomorrow."

"Not before you sing me a song. A new one!"

"Well, okay," she said, and she leaned against the door and tapped her foot on the floor. Then she sang:

I saw a little birdie come hop-hop-hop.
So I said little birdie, "will you stop-stop-stop?"
I was going to the window to say, "How do you do?"
And he shook his little feathers and away he flew.

"Again," Jackie said. Washerwoman looked across at Mama as if for her approval. Mama smiled and nodded and Washerwoman tapped her foot and sang it again.

As Jackie leaned back against the pillows, she shook the colourful beads in her hand. Mama gave her a piece of thread and sat beside her as she strung red beads and blue, purple, yellow, pink and green on the thread. They were round and square and oblong beads, and when they were all on the string, they made a beautiful necklace.

By the time Mama had tied the beads around Jackie's neck, Daddy was back. The doctor walked stiff-legged into the room and took off his helmet, resting it on the bureau.

"Got a sick little girl here, have we?" he asked. Jackie nodded.

"Well, we'll have to do something about that." He put his hand against her forehead and flashed a quick smile. Then he opened his black bag, took out a thermometer, and slipped it in Jackie's mouth.

"How long has she been sick?" he asked Daddy. He cupped his ear with his hand and Daddy moved close to him and spoke in his ear.

"Since last night."

"Since when?"

"Last night," Daddy said.

He removed the thermometer from her mouth and looked down at it. "No fever. That's good," he said.

He lifted Jackie's blouse and moved an instrument from around his neck and put it in his ears. Then he listened to her back and chest as he told her to cough again and again. Jackie wondered how he could hear the wheezing in her chest if he couldn't hear Daddy shout.

"Got a bad mustard plaster burn, you have," he said, and he gave Mama a quick smile. "But I've heard worse wheezing. Next time mix the mustard plaster with egg whites in place of water and it won't blister her."

"That's good to know," Mama said. "Thank you."

"Do you think she got sick from too much swimming?" Daddy asked.

"Yes, I've heard worse," the Doctor replied. When he pressed on Jackie's stomach and sides, she jumped and yelled, "Ouch!"

"Aye, I know. Sore muscles. Too much coughing. We must stop the coughing. Let me see your throat." Mama handed him a spoon.

"Stick out your tongue," he said and he held it down with the spoon and looked in her throat.

"Aye, it's red, real red." He took his handkerchief from his pocket and wiped the sweat from his forehead. Then he took off his stiff white coat. His pants were held up with brown suspenders, and almost rested beneath his armpits.

Looking around the room, he said, "Too hot in here. Open the windows. She'll breathe better with fresh air."

Daddy walked toward the windows and Mama threw him a nervous glance. He opened them anyway, and soon Jackie began to feel better.

Again the doctor opened his black bag. This time he took out a bottle of tonic and handed it to Mama.

"Give her one tablespoon of this medicine three times a day," he said. "It will rid her of the cough. Bad attack of asthma, it is."

He closed his black bag, walked over to the bureau, and picked up his coat and helmet.

"May I go out and play tomorrow?" Jackie asked him.

"Of course, you've been a good girl," the doctor replied. As he stood by the door, he waved to Jackie with his helmet. He smiled once more and said, "Yes, I'd say you've been a very good girl, you have."

13

THE SHIP BENEATH THE SEA

Jackie picked up a handful of marbles and her taw and drew a circle beneath the pear tree. She would practice alone. The previous day she had lost several of her prized marbles to Rita when they had played for *keeps*. Now Jackie held the huge marble that was her taw between her thumb and forefinger and practiced shooting the marbles out of the circle.

Rita came by and inquired if Judy and Jackie could go for a canoe ride. As Jackie picked up her marbles and ran inside, she met Daddy by the door.

"May I go, Daddy, please may I go out in the canoe?" Jackie asked.

"I worry when you girls go out in boats," Daddy said.

"Oh please, Daddy, please let me go," Jackie pleaded.

Daddy thought for a moment and then he said, "If Judy goes, then you may go."

She did not understand why Daddy thought she would be safer if Judy went too. After all, she was taller than Judy and had longer legs!

However, Judy was older and Daddy trusted her to hold the boat steady. He said Jackie was too young to handle a canoe and a paddle.

Soon the three girls stood on the shore at White Hall Bay. Anchored a short distance away the canoe pitched and rocked slightly. Jackie had not told Daddy that they planned to borrow Tom Salt Water's canoe without permission.

They pulled the boat to shore, and Jackie and Judy climbed in and pulled up the anchor.

"Hold the boat steady while I unhitch the rope from the shore and jump in," Rita said. Soon the canoe glided over the clear water and she grabbed a paddle and headed out of the bay.

Since there were only two wooden seats, Jackie sat in the middle of the canoe. The seats were made from flat pieces of wood and fitted, one at the back, the other at the front. Rita sat on the back seat and Judy on the front one and now they each began to paddle.

"Your job will be to bail the water out as fast as it splashes in," Judy said to Jackie.

"Okay. I don't mind. Of course I would rather paddle."

"Then we'll trade seats," Judy said. The canoe rocked as the sisters traded seats. Jackie began paddling and the boat moved in circles.

"What am I doing wrong?" she asked.

"You have to paddle first on one side, then on the other, to keep the boat straight." Rita glanced at Judy and they laughed.

Jackie gave Judy back her seat and paddle. Tears stung her eyes, but she didn't cry. She picked up the calabash and began to bail the water from the boat.

Judy and Rita knew how to move the paddles so that the boat went where they wanted it to go. But they were older, Jackie thought. It was okay. She had not yet learned that.

They paddled fast and headed for deep water. Jackie's eyes scanned the seashore. She saw Daddy's store with its gray walls and zinc roof.

"I see Washerwoman leaving the store with a bottle of kerosene in her hand," Jackie said.

"And I see Daddy watching from a window in the printing shop," Judy added.

Jackie waved to Daddy and he waved his white handkerchief. He stood there a long time until finally she could see him no more, but she knew he was probably still watching.

"There's Hogsty Bay," Rita said. Children waved to them from the bay, where they were swimming.

"Give us a canoe ride," the children yelled as they beckoned them to come in closer. But Judy shifted the paddle to the left side of the boat and it moved to deeper water. Straight out they went, farther and farther. Then Judy and Rita rested their paddles inside the canoe.

"Look down, Jackie," Judy said. "Tell us what you see."

The canoe rocked as Jackie peered over the side.

"Oh, a ship! A huge ship!" Jackie said.

She wanted to see it better so she picked up the water glass from beside her. She fitted the square wooden box, with the opening at the top, against her face. The bottom, made of clear glass, she pressed against the water.

"It is so-o-o pretty down there," she said, her voice muffled as she spoke into the water glass. "The broken ship is resting on the sand, one half pointing one way and the other half over from it. I can see *Calle* written on the side. Poor *Calle*. Washerwoman would like to see this." Jackie remembered that the ship had gone down the previous year, sinking during a storm. She recalled Washerwoman singing as the ship went down:

Calle burning, Calle burning,
Look yonder, look yonder,
Fire-fire, fire-fire,
And we have no water.

She must remember what she saw so she could tell Washerwoman about it.

Then her mind snapped back to the ship below her. "I see huge groupers swimming in and out of the ship, and porgy fish sticking their pug noses against its side. They look like they're eating something along the outside of the boat. Huge rocks around it are covered with seaweed and black sea eggs." A popeyed squirrel fish swam by only a short distance beneath them, and Jackie smiled as his enormous eyes peeped at her through the water glass.

"Well, we won't need to look through the water glass," Rita said. "Jackie has seen it all out loud for us." They laughed again and Jackie's feelings were hurt, but she did not let them know. She had learned that being picked on was the price she must pay for tagging along with bigger girls.

Judy fitted her face against the water glass. She just stared into it for a while. Then she said, "Rita, there's an anchor! Looks half the size of our canoe and resting on the bottom. Take a look." She handed the water glass to her.

Rita had scarcely begun peering through it when she gasped. "I see something strange down there. Something big and black like an overgrown frog."

"Are you kidding?" Judy asked.

"No, here!"

Jackie took the water glass from her, fitting her face against it. "Oh, she's right. A strange looking being is swimming in and out of the ship. It put something down on the sand. Looks like a wheel. I want to go home! Take me home!"

"Let me see," Judy said, and she peered through the water glass. "My goodness, it's a monster."

"Let me out of here! No, take me home!" Jackie said.

"Don't panic and turn the canoe over," Judy said. "It's a diver, silly. He's salvaging the parts of the ship that are still good."

Jackie had never seen a diver before, or his black suit, or the flaps on his feet, or his goggles. She was glad that Judy knew what the strange being was. Streams of bubbles rose to the surface and the older girls picked up the paddles and steered the canoe toward the shore.

Suddenly, they stopped paddling.

"There it is," Judy said. "Grandma Achie's head — the biggest round rock in the harbour."

"Wow, it's bigger than I imagined," Jackie said. *She was remembering the time that Judy and Rita swam out to this rock and were chased by a shark.*

They moved on and wings flapped nearby as man-of-war birds circled the canoe. Jackie watched sea grape trees wave their large, fan-shaped leaves in the breeze. The popnut trees, with their yellow bell-shaped flowers, swayed back and forth.

Children no longer swam in Hogsty Bay, and Jackie missed their friendly waving hands. A car drove lazily down the road, coasting as slowly as the canoe.

Then, Jackie saw Daddy's store and the sparkling white printing shop and the house. She watched as Daddy came to the unscreened window. He shaded his eyes with his hand and waved to them.

Soon the canoe was anchored safely in White Hall Bay, its rope tied to the boat, the iron peg holding it securely to the iron shore. Jackie hurried home, conscious of her waterlogged fingers. Just the same she was anxious to tell Daddy and Mama what she had seen.

Later that evening, as they sat in the swing on the porch, Jackie related every detail of the canoe trip to them and to little brother John. She told them about the pug nose porgies that ate the seaweed from the side of the wrecked ship.

"But the strangest thing, Daddy, was the frogman," Jackie said. "He wore fins on his feet, goggles over his eyes, and a tank strapped to his back. He swam in and out of the ship like a fish."

Even before Jackie could finish telling her story, she looked up, and the frogman was walking by in his black suit. His fins were in one hand, his goggles in the other and the big steering wheel that had lain at the bottom of the sea was over his shoulder.

"Hotdog!," Daddy said. He laughed and laughed and his gold tooth sparkled in the evening sunlight.

14

SHE'S NOT OLD

Jackie ran barefoot in the sandyard and called to April as she walked down the footpath.

"Can you come over and play in our little house under the tangerine tree?" April asked.

"Yes," Jackie said. She climbed over the fence and the two friends skipped down the pathway until they stood in front of their little house. The thatch roof rippled in the breeze, and clusters of bright orange-coloured tangerines hung from the branches of the tree.

Jackie and April picked handfuls of tangerines. Inside their house, they ate until they couldn't eat another bite.

Then Jackie swept the sand floor. April wiped the little dishes and put them back in the box, then took them out and wiped them once more.

"I can't believe that summer is over," Jackie said. "Three more days until school starts again."

"Yeah, but I'm excited about going back to school," April said.

"Me too. Kinda," Jackie said. "We've had a good time. I wonder if our naseberry gum has hardened on the tree trunk where we cut slits to make bubble gum from the tree trunk milk."

"Let's go and see," April said.

The two girls climbed the naseberry tree and checked the sun-dried milk that had oozed from the slits they had cut. They pulled it from the tree and began chewing it.

"Wish we had some brown sugar and a drop of peppermint to mix with it," April said. "It's kind of tasteless this way."

"I don't mind," Jackie told her. "It's bubble gum and that's all that I care about. Watch!" Jackie blew such a big bubble that it almost covered her face when it popped.

April had a scowl on her face. "I can't enjoy it for thinking how many lizards might have crawled over it. Wish I had waited and washed mine."

"Not me," Jackie said. "Mine's just fine," and she giggled.

They climbed down from the naseberry tree and ran to blow bubbles in April's front yard. Cousin Melinda, April's next-door neighbour, came to the fence and called to Jackie.

"I've made something for your Daddy. Would you take it home to him?"

"Yes ma'am," Jackie said. So she walked the short distance to Cousin Melinda's kitchen door.

"Come in, child," Cousin Melinda said.

Jackie stood in the doorway and hesitated to go further. The unpainted kitchen floor had been scrubbed until it was spotless. In one corner she saw a tiny homemade table with two matching chairs.

A shelf along the wall held five bottles. Jackie saw flour in the first bottle, then red beans, brown sugar, corn meal, and the last bottle held coffee beans. Beside that jar was a tiny coffee grinder with a handle to grind the coffee.

Jackie loved this little kitchen, where Cousin Melinda twirled around in her full skirt that almost touched the floor. Her gray hair was pulled back in a knot on the back of her head and her eyes twinkled when she smiled.

"Did you get a new caboose, Cousin Melinda?" Jackie asked.

"Yes," she said. "Bugger finally made me a new one. See, he put this shelf beneath for the pots and pans."

"Yes, I like it," Jackie said.

She looked at every detail of that caboose. The oblong wooden box stood on legs in the corner. The huge box was filled halfway up with sand. Little sticks had been placed on the sand and three iron rods stretched across the width and rested on the frame.

"Wait just a minute while I stir my beans," Cousin Melinda said. Straddling the three rods, a pot boiled. She stirred it with a wooden spoon. An open window beside it took the smoke outside.

Cousin Melinda's skirt swished as she took an iron skillet off the fire. She sang, *Just to be a child again.* Jackie knew almost instantly what she had cooked.

"I made a bammy for your Daddy today," she said.

"Oh, good," Jackie said. "Daddy really likes them and you're the only person I know that still makes them."

"Don't know why," Cousin Melinda said. "They're easy enough to make. I grate the cassava, sprinkle it with salt, and squeeze it until it is as round and flat as a flapjack. Then I cook it in my iron skillet until it browns."

"Daddy will be proud to hear that I know how to make bammy," Jackie said.

Cousin Melinda smiled as she tied the bammy in a clean cloth so that Jackie could take it home without getting burned. Swinging with each step, she felt the heat rise from inside the soft cloth.

It was almost dinnertime, so Jackie hid the bammy in the kitchen to surprise Daddy.

As she moved into the house, she saw Mama sewing a button on a royal blue jumper. Beside her was the pale blue blouse to be worn with it. She was still making school uniforms.

Jackie sat beside her and gave her a hug. She smelled good, like fresh roses. She had been sewing almost every day for the past week. She said she wanted each of her children to have at least three school uniforms to begin the school year. John's khaki uniforms were spread on the bed. It would be his first year in school.

"I just sewed the last button on the last uniform," Mama said, and she smiled. Jackie knew that Mama had sewn each stitch with love.

Baw Baw called them to dinner and Jackie was excited when she smelled the noon meal. There was turtle meat and rice, baked ripe plantain and steamed breadfruit. Jackie could just taste Cousin Melinda's bammy with that dinner.

Daddy sat at the head of the table and everyone bowed their heads. Then he prayed:
> *For what we're about to receive, Oh Lord,*
> *Make us humbly thankful. Amen.*

Jackie asked to be excused and went for the bammy. She unwrapped it and put it beside Daddy's plate. He laughed as he said, "Bless you, Cousin Melinda." Then he broke it and gave Jackie a piece. No one else cared for the coarse, bread-like taste of bammy, but it was a real treat for Daddy and Jackie.

As they ate, Jackie asked Daddy about something that concerned her.

"Cousin Melinda is really old, isn't she, Daddy?" Jackie asked. "How old do you think she is?"

"In her eighties," Daddy said. "But you don't count age with years. Some people grow old because they don't have a dream. Did you see a sparkle in Cousin Melinda's eyes, Coo-Coo?"

"Yes Daddy, I did," Jackie told him.

"Then she's not old," Daddy said.

Jackie always felt better when Daddy explained things to her. She said no more, but when the meal was over, Daddy cleared his throat and said, "I know a little poem that reminds me of Cousin Melinda, and it goes like this:
> *Age is a quality of time.*
> *If you have left your dreams behind*
> *And hope is cold,*
> *If you no longer look ahead,*
> *If your ambitions fires are dead,*
> *Then you're old.*

But if from life you take the best,
If in life you keep the jest
And love you hold,
No matter how quickly the years go by,
No matter how fast the birthdays fly,
You're not old.

"Thank you, Daddy. She's not old!" Later that evening, Jackie sat on the rocky shore behind Daddy's store. She watched the sun turn red and light up the blue sky. Like a big ball of fire, it finally disappeared below the horizon.

Sometimes as she watched the clear Caribbean Sea wash gently against the seashore, sentences formed in her head and she jotted them down on paper.

Today, she thought of Cousin Melinda. Jackie knew that Daddy was right when he said that she wasn't old. But eighty still seemed old to Jackie. She recalled Cousin Melinda's song: *Just to be a child again.* She remembered Cousin Melinda's kitchen and was wondering how she would fit into Heaven with its gates of pearl and streets of gold. She pulled her tiny notebook and pencil from her pocket and wrote: *This one is for you, Cousin Melinda.*

A familiar dream came back last night
To gladden my heart once more.
In child-like glee it seems I heard
The waves along the shore.
Someday I want to go to Heaven,
And I know up there 'tis grand
I hope a sign above my mansion reads,
"You're on the Island of Cayman."

Jackie was excited as she crossed the street to show it to Daddy and Mama. She put her own tune to the words she had written, and she skipped and sang:

'Cause Heaven wouldn't seem like Heaven
If Cayman isn't there,
The sparkling Caribbean, beaches beyond compare,
Coconut trees that sway in the breeze,
Familiar faces everywhere.
Heaven wouldn't seem like Heaven
If Cayman isn't there.

Hammocks tied beneath fruit trees
Move at a gentle pace
Little children swinging in them
Have a smile upon each face
High up in the banana trees
Birds sing their merry songs
How could this Island Time Forgot
Not be viewed by heavenly throngs?

IN THE RAYS OF A CAYMAN SUNSET

By
Jackie Bodden

Illustrated by Susan Acree

CONTENTS

1. JANE PIC-PIC — 201
2. THE TALKING ICE CREAM FREEZER — 208
3. THE TURTLE WITH A TEAR IN HIS EYE — 213
4. THOSE HAPPY SCHOOL DAYS — 219
5. FRIGHTENING THINGS — 225
6. THE BODDEN TOWN GARDEN PARTY — 230
7. THE BELL RANG ONLY ONCE — 237
8. A DOVE NAMED HIPPITY HOP — 241
9. A CAYMAN COWBOY — 245
10. SKINNY-LEE-LEE — 250
11. REMEMBRANCE DAY THROUGH A CHILD'S EYES — 255
12. COWBOYS AND INDIANS — 260
13. SHIP AHOY! — 265
14. TWO CAYMAN BROTHERS REMEMBER — 271
15. A SUNDAY EVENING WALK — 274
16. A SCHOONER IS LAUNCHED — 280

To My Children
Ronnie, Lisa, Cindy, Gina
And Grandchildren
Brandon, Caitlyn, Madelyn,
Laura, Meagan, Rachel
With Love

1

JANE PIC-PIC

Cayman with its sparsely populated towns enjoyed a kind of peace that comes only from knowing almost every Island family. This allowed the children to run free, though filled with curiosity about the few people who lived like hermits. One such person was Ms. Jane Pic-Pic.

"Listen," Lil Go-Go said. "Ms. Jane Pic-Pic is playing the piano!"

"Let's go nearer and try to see her," Jackie told her. "I've never really seen her up close before."

Red and black curly beans, peeping through half-open pods, lined the footpath that led to her house, along with jump-up-and-kiss-me flowers. Soon the footpath ended, and before them lay a well-kept flower garden outlined with pink conch shells.

Set back a distance, the old house sat with its faded green shutters and paint-stripped wooden walls. The bare wood looked gray, and the tin roof glistened in the sunlight.

"I've seen inside her house before. I walk this way going to school every day," Lil Go-Go said.

The music drifted through the air. *Jane Pic-Pic, Jane Pic-Pic,* it seemed to say.

"I just want to see her one time," Jackie said.

"Quiet," Lil Go-Go told her. "You'll let her hear us."

Jackie placed her hands on the windowsill and her bare feet climbed the walls. Then, she got her first glimpse around the parlour.

"Almost bare, isn't it?" Jackie whispered to her friend. "Except for the old piano and rocking chair, but she's pretty, isn't she? Old, but pretty, with her hair all up in curlers."

"Be quiet," Lil Go-Go said. "Give me a turn." As she climbed, her hand slipped and she fell.

The music stopped and Ms. Jane Pic-Pic hurried to the door. "Who's there? Anybody there?" she asked.

Jackie and Lil Go-Go hid in the crawl space beneath the house. Surely they would be safe there. But then they saw them—big spiders weaving their cobwebs, and an ugly black centipede with its many legs.

They scuffled to get away from there, but they heard footsteps and watched as someone in a long white dress came around the corner toward them. When she got to the window she stooped and peeped beneath the house.

"Come out of there," she said. "Get yourselves out of there."

Jackie's heart pounded and she could hardly breathe. Edging her way from beneath the house, she tried to escape. But something was holding her back! Her dress was twisted around the lady's hand.

"Where do you think you're going?" she asked, her false teeth clacking.

"Why, home!" Jackie told her.

"Well, not so fast. What were you doing looking in my window?"

"I'm sorry," Jackie said. "I only wanted to see where the music was coming from. Just passing by."

"And you," she pointed a bony finger at Lil Go-Go. "I see you around here a lot, walking past my house."

"Yes, ma'am," Lil Go-Go said.

Jackie was tugging on her dress now, but it wouldn't pull loose.

"Please let me go," she pleaded. "I need to go home." Tears streamed down Jackie's face but she did not cry.

Ms. Jane Pic-Pic took a soft handkerchief from her pocket and wiped the tears. "Don't be afraid of me," she said. "I won't hurt you. I like children. You know I planned to have some myself. Even made some little clothes."

She released Jackie's dress and her eyes stared way off into the woods beyond her yard. "Yes, I wanted children like you. Had a husband too but I wouldn't go away with him. Couldn't leave my mother. He left home and never came back. Never once came back!"

"I'm sorry," Jackie said. "Real sorry."

Ms. Jane Pic-Pic sighed a loud sigh. "Don't be, child. That was a long, long time ago. Now if you would like, I'll play a different tune."

The old lady stood and slowly climbed the steps. Jackie still wanted to run, but Lil Go-Go held her back. "Wait, let's listen," she said.

Peeling through the air, a frolicking tune came from inside the house. Jackie and Lil Go-Go joined hands and swung around and around just outside her garden.

"Listen," Lil Go-Go said. "She's singing." From through the open window, they heard a crackling little voice:

To all you young men who have worrying wives,
A piece of advice I would give.
If you follow my ADVICE,
You'll have peace on this earth while you live.
You don't interfere, whatever she do
You just let her have all the say.
For instance, supposing your wife says to you
"I think we'll go boating today."
If the Missus wants to go, let her go, let her go
If the Missus wants to row, let her row.
Ten to one, she'll get upset
If you watch her going down
So don't interrupt her, let her drown, let her drown.

Lil Go-Go laughed until she fell amidst a cluster of orchids. "Sing us some more," she yelled.

"No more," a voice behind them said. "Look at you girls. All sweaty and your faces streaked with dirt." It was Baw Baw. She had cooked for Jackie's family for many years.

"Why are you going home so early?" Jackie asked looking down. "I'm not standing on my shadow, so it's not noon yet."

"'Cause nobody is hungry. Cooked all that food and nobody eating! Good food with no seasoning! Couldn't put no salt pork in the fish dinner I cooked in coconut milk gravy. Couldn't put no ham in the beans. Duppy dinner, that's what I cooked today."

"But why?" Lil Go-Go asked.

Baw Baw wiped beads of sweat from her face with her skirt. "'Cause Nurse Donna is there. And she don't eat no salt pork or ham."

"Nurse Donna?" Jackie asked. "The b-a-b-y?"

Baw Baw looked beyond Jackie to Ms. Jane Pic-Pic who was standing in the doorway. "A little girl," she crooned. "Come home from the hospital this morning."

"A little girl," Ms. Jane Pic-Pic echoed. "A baby girl!"

Jackie's long legs ran toward home, her hair blowing wildly behind her. Breathlessly, she arrived at Mama's room. Nurse Donna blocked her way, a pink bundle in her arms.

"Shush! Come see what the stork brought you," she said. "For the next nine days, while I'm here taking care of your mother and this baby, I'll not have you running wild or making noise. But come now and I'll show you your baby sister." She bent forward and unwrapped the blanket.

Jackie's breath caught in her throat. "Oh, she's so beautiful," she whispered. "My baby sister, and lucky to be born in the little new hospital. If it had been built earlier, I could have been born there too, instead of at home."

"Don't be silly," Nurse Donna told her. "You did okay."

That evening as Jackie rocked in the swing on the porch with her older sisters, Jane and Judy, and her little brother, John, Ms. Jane Pic-Pic rounded the street corner. Slid halfway down her nose was a pair of round-rim glasses, and little kiss curls covered her forehead. She moved slowly, holding on to the fence. Jackie thought she was going to Daddy's store across the street, but when she arrived at the gate, she stopped and turned into the yard. Jackie jumped from the swing as she came up the porch steps.

"I brought this for the baby," she said, holding out a crumpled brown paper bag. Her voice trembled, but she was smiling.

Inside was a pair of crocheted baby shoes, all yellowed and spotted with age.

"Oh, thank you, they're so lovely," Jackie said and she reached up and hugged her new friend.

2

THE TALKING ICE CREAM FREEZER

"Did anyone tell you we're going to make ice cream?" Jackie asked Washerwoman.

"My-oh-my, I bet it'll be good," Washerwoman said, "Whatever it is."

"I only ate it once," Jackie told her. "Two days ago. It was as sweet as a sweetsop and as smooth as young coconut cream."

"Then it's good," Washerwoman said.

"Well, hurry and finish scrubbing those pots, so we can make it. Here, let me help you."

Jackie grabbed a dried breadfruit leaf, wet it, and dipped it in ashes. She scrubbed and scrubbed the bottoms of the pots."

"Looks like you've done this before," Washerwoman told her.

"I have. In the little house under the tangerine tree," Jackie replied. "I washed lots of pots."

From the back door Mama's call came, "I've mixed the ice cream and I need someone to turn the freezer."

Washerwoman washed the ashes off the pots and left them to dry on the table under the avocado pear tree. "I declare, I can see my own smile in them," she said, drying her hands on her skirt.

Straddling the platform, in the breezeway between the house and the kitchen, Jackie saw the ice cream freezer that Daddy had given Mama for Christmas only a few days earlier. Mama plunged an ice pick into the big block of ice from the ice plant. She picked up the chips of ice and piled them in the ice cream freezer. When it could hold no more, she sprinkled coarse salt all over the ice and covered it with a burlap sack.

Mama smiled as she looked down at the freezer. "I hope your father is as happy with the radio that I bought him for Christmas from the mail-order catalog."

Jackie reached up and hugged her. "I'm sure he is."

Washerwoman turned the handle and laughed. "I can do that."

"Give me the first turn," Jackie told her. "When I get tired, I'll give it to you."

Washerwoman sat on the ground, smoothing the sand with her hand. "Tell me 'bout you," she said. "What do you think 'bout all the goings-on around town these days?"

"Isn't it exciting? I mean, the movie theatre that they're going to build in town, and a foreigner has bought land on the Seven-Mile Beach to build a hotel. And guess what else they're doing?"

"What?"

"They're clearing land to build an airstrip for planes that can land on the ground."

"Oh my," Washerwoman said. "I wouldn't give you two pence for the young brains around with all their newfangled ideas."

She stood up and began turning the handle on the ice cream freezer. Jackie sat on the wooden walkway. A cool north wind whipped past them.

"Thank goodness your grandfather built the kitchen separate from the house," Washerwoman said. "That way the house is cool even when the kitchen is hot. I like this breezeway."

"Me too," Jackie told her.

Bang-bang, sounded the hammers in the distance. *Bang, bang, bang.*

"Just listen!" Washerwoman whispered. "Can't hear yourself think with all these new houses going up. That Mr. Southward is about to call every Island man away to work on his ships."

"Daddy calls it progress," Jackie told her.

Washerwoman smiled.

Suddenly she jumped back and pointed her finger at water pouring from the side of the ice cream freezer.

"I broke it," she said. "I must 'ave turned it too hard. Go get me some brown paper."

Jackie ran to the kitchen and came back with a brown paper bag. Washerwoman quickly tore the bag, twisted the paper and plugged up the hole.

"There," she said. "That should do it." And she continued turning.

From somewhere a voice said, "If you wished the weather today would be sunny, you got your wish."

Washerwoman quit turning the handle and walked in circles around the freezer. "Who dat?" she asked, pointing a finger at the freezer. "Who dat talking to me?" She looked up at the blue sky. "Sunny, all right," she said. "But the wind is cool."

"The court case is still in progress," the voice continued. "If the jury finds Mr. Summers guilty, he could go to prison."

"Oh no! Poor old Mr. Man-Man Sums. Going to jail! But what did he do? I didn't know he did anything bad in his life." She wiped the tears from her eyes before stepping aside for Cory to begin turning the freezer. Cory was cooking for the family while Baw Baw took a week off.

Jackie heard Daddy's footsteps as he left the dining room and walked toward the front door. The voice they had been hearing faded as Daddy walked away.

Washerwoman plopped down on the ground, her dusty toes wiggling in the sand, her ear beside the freezer.

"Talk to her," she said, shaking her finger at it. "You talked to me, now talk to Cory!"

Cory sighed.

Washerwoman shuffled, stirring the dust and crushing the yellow and purple crocus flowers around her.

"You need to turn the handle faster to get the machine to talk," she said.

"It's hard to turn now. I can't go any faster," Cory told her.

Washerwoman closed her eyes and smiled. "Who dat, who dat talked to me?" she asked the ice cream freezer again. "Let me hear you talk again."

Just then, Daddy walked by, with his radio in his hand, his gold tooth shining in the sunlight. "Hotdog!" he said. "An ice cream freezer and a radio all in the same Christmas!"

"That ends today's news," the radio said.

"Hear that?" Washerwoman said. "The voice moved from this machine to that one."

Jackie and Cory laughed, but Washerwoman just shook her head.

Mama came to the door to inquire about the ice cream. She checked the handle to be sure it would no longer turn.

"Get your bowls," she told them. "It's ready."

Washerwoman held out her bowl and Mama filled it with ice cream. She put one spoonful in her mouth and gagged

"Whatever is wrong?" Mama asked. "Don't you like it?"

"No ma'am," Washerwoman replied.

Mama tasted it. "Salt!" she said. "How did salt get from the ice into the ice cream?"

"I don't know," Jackie said. "The freezer broke, but Washerwoman and I fixed it. See," and she showed Mama the brown paper plug.

"Oh no," Mama said. "That hole is there to let the water and the salt out as the ice melts. But don't worry," she continued. "I'll mix up another batch and we'll have ice cream anyhow."

"My-oh-my," Washerwoman said. "So much for progress! I think I'll go home. I've had enough excitement for one day."

3

THE TURTLE WITH A TEAR IN HIS EYE

Jackie and her friends had left Papa's bay for home after swimming much too long. Her eyes burned and her fingers were all wrinkled and she was cold.

She tripped and fell when she ran into a turtle that had been placed on its back beneath the grape tree. *A turtle? How could it have gotten here?* Then she saw two other turtles.

"I'm sorry, Mr. Turtle," she heard herself say as she bent down to look at him. "I didn't mean to hurt you."

It was then that she saw it. *A tear trickled from the corner of his eye! Of course, it had to be a mistake. Who ever heard of a turtle crying?* But when that tear had hit the ground another one formed in the same eye. She tried to turn him over but he was too heavy.

"Are you hungry? I'll go and get you something to eat."

Jackie's teeth chattered as she jumped back in the sea and began pulling green moss from the big rock in the middle of the bay. Finally, when she had gathered just a little bit, she took it to him. *Now, how do you feed a*

turtle? She wondered. *I'm certainly not sticking my hand near that big mouth!*

Then she got an idea. She put the moss on a grape leaf and held it up to his mouth, but he wouldn't open it. She even tried to smear it on his mouth, but he kept it shut tight.

She hunted around and found a rusty tin can and filled it with sea water. When she had poured it over his body, the tears quit flowing. So she poured more and more water on him and his two friends.

"One of the turtles under the grape tree was crying, Mama," she said after she had crossed the road and gone home.

"Nonsense," Mama said. "Who ever heard of a turtle crying?"

"Well, I poured sea water on him and he quit crying," Jackie told her.

"Well, good," Mama said.

Baw Baw was putting supper on the table. In one hand she held a platter of fried goggle-eye fish and fritters and in the other a teapot of hot cocoa. Daddy liked tea better, so beside his plate, fever-grass had been tied in a knot and was steeping in his big cup.

"You better leave those turtles alone," Baw Baw said. "I saw you trying to turn one over. You'll get a good whipping if you let him get away."

"Tell her he's mine, Daddy," Jackie said.

"No, he's not yours," Daddy replied.

After Jackie had eaten the good supper and drunk some of Daddy's fever-grass tea, she crossed the road and visited the turtle once more. *Tomorrow I'll get some friends to help me turn him over,* she thought.

But during the night, she heard voices outside.

"May I have four pounds of turtle meat?" a voice called. "Three here!" Someone else yelled. Then another said, "I want six pounds with lots of liver."

"That's enough," a man replied. "What do you think it is? An EFELANT? I ain't but one person. Now tell me, one at a time."

Jackie sprang from her bed and ran to the window and peeped outside. A crowd of people surrounded the huge sea grape tree beside Daddy's store. A lantern hung from a branch, swaying back and forth above the heads of the people.

"What's going on?" Jackie asked Mama. And why did Daddy open the store before daylight?"

"Shush and go back to sleep. When it is morning you may go out and watch."

Jackie went back to bed, but she did not sleep. She listened and she peeped between the curtains for daylight to break. The kerosene lamp that sat in the middle of the dining table cast its dim light across the wooden floor. She heard the noises of the crowd outside, and she wanted to be where they were.

In the wee hours before dawn, she watched from the window as Mr. Jimmy Sticks rolled a barrel of kerosene oil down the middle of the marl road. He brought it to Daddy's store. Then, he capped Daddy's empty drum and Mr. Jimmy Sticks began rolling it back to town.

Finally, she got dressed and crossed the street, making her way through the crowd. Beneath the sea grape tree, the backs of two turtles lay side by side in her wheelbarrow. Horror gripped her and she felt a lump in her throat.

Daddy's store scale hung on a branch, and Mr. Jerome lifted the turtle meat from inside the turtle's back, strung it on a thatch string and weighed it on Daddy's scale.

The nerve of him butchering turtles, laying them out on our wheelbarrow and weighing the meat on Daddy's scale! And after all that, using our smoke pan to keep the mosquitoes away from him.

Here is six pounds with liver," Mr. Jerome said.

"That's mine!" a lady replied.

"If it's yours, come and get it."

"All I need now is some kerosene," she said. She stepped inside the store and placed the funnel in the quart bottle that she held. Then she slipped the bottle beneath the tap on the end of the drum, turned the handle and kerosene filled the bottle.

"Aye," she said, handing Daddy three big copper pennies. "Good times today. We'll have turtle meat for dinner."

"Yes," Daddy told her. "I'm longing to eat some myself."

Mr. Jerome wiped his face on his sleeve and turned to Skeeter. "Empty this bucket of water in the sea and go fetch me a bucket of clean sea water to wash the rest of this turtle meat in."

Dogs followed Skeeter all the way to the bay and as he went, he stuck his hand in the bucket and fed them scraps of turtle meat. They growled and snapped at each other and fought over the scraps.

"Sir," a lady said, "I'd like two pounds with lights, and could you please tell me the time?" She was unaware that Mr. Jerome had not yet learned to tell the time since receiving his watch as a Christmas present.

He stared proudly at the watch on his arm. "Nope!" he said. "I just can't figure it out. I believe Mr. Gonzales set this watch in Spanish."

Jackie could stand it no longer, she tapped Mr. Jerome on the shoulder several times until he looked at her. "What did you do with my turtle?" she cried.

"What turtle?" he asked.

"The one with the tear in his eye," Jackie told him. "He was under this tree with the others yesterday. I poured sea water on him because he was hot and crying. He was mine and I want him."

"Oh, *that* turtle," he said. "He must have been the one that got away during the night. I'm sure he's far, far out to sea by now."

"But how do you know?"

"Because when I first got here, his tracks went all the way down to the water. They're gone from here now, because there are too many footprints, but come with me."

He walked down by the bay, where nobody had yet walked in the sand and showed Jackie turtle tracks that ended at the water's edge.

4

THOSE HAPPY SCHOOL DAYS

The schoolyard stretched before her, sprinkled with boys and girls. Jackie jumped from her bicycle and leaned it against a fence post. The old United States Navy barracks, built during World War II, was now school to many Island children.

Her brother John was too young to remember the men in white uniforms with sailor caps who had once called these buildings home, but Jackie remembered having seen them. Though she had been a tiny girl at the time, she recalled jeeps packed tight with cheering men moving through the streets of George Town.

Servicemen tossed their white hats in the air. Jane and Judy twirled with excitement in the sandyard beside the marl road. Jackie recalled standing on the front porch and covering her ears with her hands to shut out the noise of the pots and pans and graters tied to the jeeps' bumpers, and the loud horns. Daddy laughed and waved his handkerchief and yelled, "Hurrah, the war is over!"

"Over?" Jackie had asked Daddy.

"Yes," Daddy said. "The men are happy because the war is over and they can go home to America."

America! Jackie had heard that word many times. It sounded far, far away.

Oh, I hope they don't take the blimp away, she remembered thinking. Each time that the big gray balloon had flown overhead, she had walked the few steps from the house to Daddy's printing shop and knocked on his window for him to see it. He had laughed and stood there and watched it with her until it was out of sight. Then he had beckoned for Mama to take her back in the house. *They just can't take my blimp away,* she remembered thinking. *They just can't!*

"And the blimp, Daddy? Will they leave the big balloon in the air?"

"Probably not," Daddy had said. "The blimp will probably go too."

Of course they had to leave the barracks! Those four wooden buildings sheltered the tiny cement building in the center of the grounds. All that excitement had taken place before Jackie was old enough to go to school. Before the empty buildings left behind by the men in uniform had been turned into Cayman Preparatory School and Cayman High School. Now, the grounds were covered once more, not with men, but with children. Laughing, yelling, happy children!

Jackie was lost in those memories of early childhood when she heard a yell, "Join our team." Kerrie Sue beckoned to her.

She ran toward the little cement building where two teams played, one on either side of it. She clasped Kerrie

Sue's hand, and they swung their arms back and forth in excitement.

"Andy-over," Curt yelled as he flung the sponge ball over the building. Ken, on the other side, caught the ball, and he rounded the corner touching everyone he could and calling, "Out. You're out. Now you're on our team." But Jackie and Kerrie Sue escaped and ran safely to the other side.

It was Jackie's turn to throw the ball over the building, and she tossed it as hard as she could. There was dead silence on the other side until someone said, "Ouch! Who hit me with de ball?"

Jackie edged her way to the corner and peeped around the side of the building just in time to see Mr. Gonzales holding one hand to the side of his face.

"Who hit me," he said. "Wis one threw de ball?"

Children scattered, moving in different directions.

"Don't know," someone yelled.

"Then I take all of you to Headmaster," he said.

The players panicked and started running; acting as if they had not been a part of the game.

"All I know is, it wasn't me," Ken murmured from a distance.

"Nor me," mumbled someone in the shuffling crowd.

Mr. Gonzales held his glasses in one hand. He moved his other hand from the side of his face where a red mark covered his cheek.

"I threw the ball," a trembling voice said and Jackie stepped forward. "But I didn't mean to hit you. I'm sorry."

"Sorry no good enough," Mr. Gonzales said, pointing a finger at Jackie. "I tell your Pappy on you. I tell him you hit me."

Tears streamed down her face, but she did not cry.

"Changed me mind," Mr. Gonzales continued. "I take you to Headmaster. I tell him you hit me." He grabbed Jackie by the scruff of her neck and marched her ahead of him to the Principle's office. She wiped the tears from her face with her sleeve.

She was quiet as Mr. Gonzales showed Mr. Trent the mark on his face and his twisted eyeglasses. "She need whipping for hitting old man," he said. "Whip her good."

Mr. Trent turned pale. "Do you have anything to say?" he asked, his eyes fixed on Jackie's face.

"Yes sir," she told him. "I'm sorry. I didn't know he was crossing the schoolyard when I threw the andy-over ball to the other side of the building. It was an accident."

"I see," he said. Then he turned to Mr. Gonzales. "I'll take care of it," he told him.

Just as happy Mr. Gonzales left the office, Curt ran breathlessly up to Mr. Trent. "The old cow is out of the grass-piece again, and she's running loose behind the prep school building. Little children are crying and panicking."

"Not again!" Mr. Trent said.

"But that's not all," Curt told him. "A bunch of girls crawled between the barb wire fence into Cutty bush, and they're picking green mangoes."

"Oh no!" Mr. Trent said, and he walked toward the door. Then he turned around. "You may go now," he told Jackie. "I have bigger things to attend to."

Just then the school bell rang, and Jackie ran toward her classroom. She felt in the pocket of her school uniform blouse for the piece of twisted brown paper containing salt. *There would be no green mangoes passed around today!* But she had the salt! All Island children knew that green mangoes were no good without salt.

As Jackie walked through the door, she tossed the twisted brown paper into the trashcan, because she also knew that salt was no good without green mangoes!

5

FRIGHTENING THINGS

Jackie leaned her bicycle against a tree and ran toward the haunted house.

"Want to play a game of rounder?" Autumn asked.

"Sure," Jackie replied. She looked to the north, and in the distance she saw Daddy wave to her from the printing shop window. She was almost surprised that he didn't beckon for her to come home and change out of her school uniform.

"She can join my team," Rita yelled.

"No! You already have one too many. She's with us," Judy told her.

Jackie glanced toward the front porch that covered half the length of the haunted house. A screechy swing rocked back and forth in the wind, with no one in it.

Shading the house from the sun, a big guinep tree spread its branches everywhere. Off to one side fat caterpillars crawled on a jasmine tree all covered with pink flowers.

Jackie and her friends had inched their way up to the porch many times and looked through the front window, but it was much too frightening to think about. She always saw that big shiny eye that she was so afraid of.

Even now, it was scary playing rounder in the front yard of the haunted house. But she knew she could stay and play or be left out of the game.

Then a ball veered overhead and landed right into Jackie's hand.

"Good catch," Judy yelled. "Our inning."

Judy's team lined up for their turn at bat.

Autumn hit the ball far over the heads of the fielders.

"Run," Jane yelled. "You can make a home run," but the other team threw her out at third.

Troy was next in line. He threw the sponge ball in the air and hit it as hard as he could with his open hand, then hurried and got on base.

Suddenly, players scattered in every direction, running and screaming. Jackie turned her head just in time to see something chasing them around the yard. Wrapped in green with a hood that left the face only partly in view, the thing staggered about the yard, growling and dragging chains. The mouth looked all twisted and gnarled, and one arm reached out from beneath the blanket.

Jackie ran but something very cold moved beneath her collar and scratched her neck. She screamed, still feeling those claws wiggle.

"Help me, I think a rolling-calf has caught me, and he's clawing my neck," she said.

"There's no such thing as a rolling-calf!" Judy scolded, running to keep up with her. "You're okay, the thing didn't even touch you."

"Yes, it did," Jackie screamed. "A duppy or something is pinching my back right now. He's alive. He's moving down my back. Get him off me." She was tearing off her clothes now, buttons popping like popcorn from her school uniform. She had to stop this creepy, crawly thing from biting her.

She fell to the ground, but Judy picked her up and brushed her knees.

Anna caught up with her. "Don't be scared," she said. "That was just my Dad. He wanted to play a joke on us so he wrapped himself in an army blanket and turned his false teeth upside down. I promise it was just my Dad."

Jackie shoved her away and continued running. "Don't hold me back, 1 have to get home to Daddy and Mama."

Finally she ran for the bay, jumped into the cool, clear water, swam around a minute or two, and headed for home, still screaming, "The thing is biting me."

Daddy hurried from the store and caught her as she ran through the gate.

"What's happened to her?" he asked Judy.

"She thinks a rolling-calf is biting her."

"Good grief, Al-Al, help me," Daddy said.

He held Jackie and Mama unbuttoned the school uniform tunic at the waist. A half-dead, fat caterpillar fell to the porch floor and feebly crawled in circles.

"See," Daddy told her. "There is no such thing as a rolling-calf or duppy either. It was just a caterpillar."

"That makes it almost worse," Jackie said.

Daddy held her until finally she stopped sobbing. Then he picked up the caterpillar from the floor and flung it as far toward the sea as he could. His face was white now and his lips almost blue.

"Whoever did this knew that she was deathly afraid of caterpillars."

Mama gently pulled Jackie's blouse up revealing caterpillar scratches all over her back.

"This is no joke," Daddy said. "Who did this?" he asked.

Children scattered in every direction yelling "Not me," or "It wasn't me."

"Well, someone did," Daddy said.

Finally a small voice said, "It was me, but I didn't mean to hurt her."

"But you did!" Daddy said, and he sent Judy inside the house.

For many days, Jackie refused to pass the haunted house unless someone was with her. Finally one day she saw a truck unloading furniture and strange children playing in the yard.

That night she made almond seed and brown sugar candy, and the next day she took it with her to the haunted house. A girl about her own age met her. She had blonde hair and blue eyes and a big smile. Jackie handed her the candy, and the two girls giggled as they went inside the house.

Her mother welcomed Jackie and told her that Barbara would begin school the next day.

Jackie looked around the parlour. Whatever she had seen through the window all those many times was now gone.

"When you first came here, was there something white beside that window?" Jackie asked Barbara.

"I wonder why everybody keeps asking me that?" she said. "There was an old rocking chair all covered with a white sheet and cobwebs; clusters of cobwebs that made a big circle and went all the way up to the ceiling."

"Really?" Jackie asked, remembering the sunlight shining on it. "You mean it wasn't an eye or a duppy, or a rolling-calf?"

"No, it wasn't," Barbara told her and the two girls laughed and ate almond seed candy and rocked on the screechy porch swing.

6

THE BODDEN TOWN GARDEN PARTY

"Looky yonder," Jackie yelled as Daddy's car pulled up in the Manse yard in Bodden Town.

"Listen to her, Mama," Jane said. "She's starting to talk just like Washerwoman."

"Not true," Jackie told her.

"Look there!" Mama corrected her.

"Yes, ma'am. Look there, at all those laughing children."

The car stopped, and Daddy pulled his cap down on his forehead. "Mind your manners, children!" he said. "All of you."

"Yes, sir," they echoed.

Jackie ran from the car toward a group of children standing in a big circle around a tall pole. The boys faced one direction, and the girls were headed the other way. Each child held onto a ribbon attached to the top of the pole. The girls wore dresses of many colours while the boys were in khakis, and the ribbons they held made Jackie think of all the colours of a rainbow.

Oh, how she wanted to join them, but there were no ribbons left. She looked from face to face and realized that she did not know even one boy or girl in the circle. So she stood on the outside and looked on.

At least she was glad that Mama had dressed her for the occasion! She had wondered why Mama was sewing for the past couple of weeks. *She must have attended a Garden Party in the past,* Jackie thought.

She glanced down at the blue, pink, and yellow striped skirt that she was wearing. A wide yellow sash held the ruffled pink blouse in place at the waist. And her sisters, Jane and Judy, wore outfits just like hers, but in different colours.

A girl waved to her from the circle and Jackie placed her hand on her chest and asked, "Me?"

The girl nodded and she ran toward her.

"Hi, my name is Nessa, we can both hold onto this ribbon," she said. "It'll be fun."

"Oh! Such a pretty name! My name is Jackie. What are we going to do?"

"We're going to plait the ribbon around the pole," was her reply.

"But I don't know how," Jackie told her.

"You can do it," she said. "It's easy to learn, and it's fun."

Just then the music started and the children took a bow and moved forward. Jackie and Nessa twirled on the outside of the first boy they met, then Nessa steered her to the inside of the next boy, and back to the outside of the third, and on and on they danced.

When all players had only a small piece of ribbon left, they stopped.

"Oh-h-h-h!" Jackie gasped as she looked at the pole all covered with the plaited ribbons.

"What do we do next?" she asked.

"We'll turn and go the other way and that will unwind the ribbon and leave the pole free for others to begin again," Nessa said.

When at last they had unwound the ribbons, Jackie felt dizzy, but that was a small price to pay for so much fun.

The band played again and other girls and boys twirled and parents laughed and clapped, and babies in their arms cooed.

Jackie wandered past a table all covered with crocheted doilies and runners and embroidered pillowcases, the patterns sewn with every colour of embroidery thread that she had ever seen. She motioned for Mama to come and see.

"Would you please buy this piece of crochet for me?" she asked Mama, pointing to a pink-and-white runner. "See, the words *HOME SWEET HOME* have been crocheted in the center of it."

"It is unusually pretty," Mama said, "but I don't think you need anything so expensive. I taught you how to crochet, and you helped to make Joy's baby clothes, all fancy with crocheted lace. And you're good at it."

"But I need it for a pattern, Mama. I want to make some just like it for gifts for people."

Mama shook her head *No,* so Jackie moved on.

In the distance, John rode a pony around the yard, and Jackie wanted to ride it too. She had never ridden a pony before.

When John's ride was over, Jackie held out her money and straddled the pony, but as it trotted away, her feet dangled on the ground. The owner said he was sorry but she would have to get off. *If only my legs were not so long,* she thought. But then she saw Nessa coming toward her.

"Come with me," Nessa said and she held onto Jackie's hand and walked over to a table all covered with candy. There were tamarind balls, almond seed candy, red-and-white coconut candy, and twisted peppermints made in Nessa's kitchen.

"This is my Mom's table," Nessa said. "She made all this candy. She wants to give you some. What kind would you like?"

She chose the red-and-white coconut square, and nothing had ever tasted so good.

As they ate candy, they watched the adults dance the quadrille. Oh, how fast they moved those feet! Jackie began jigging the way they did, and by the time it was over she pretty much knew how to dance it.

The band stopped playing, and Daddy stood talking with the man that played the accordion. Jackie had seen him before many times when he rode his bicycle down from his job in George Town to visit Daddy. They were laughing and Daddy's gold tooth glistened in the evening sunlight.

Sitting on a stump beside them, the fiddle player shined his fiddle, and next to him, a man stuck his mouth organ in his pocket, while another laid his grater and fork on the ground beside him, covered his face with his hat, and fell asleep.

All too soon, it was time to go home, but Jackie asked for one last time around the Plait Pole. When it was over, she told Nessa goodbye and headed for the car.

Mama had bought cassava cake and plantain tarts and a large bowl of cooked conchs and sea-pie to take home. And peeping through cellophane paper, Jackie saw a china doll that Mama had bought for baby sister, Joy. She was wearing a gorgeous embroidered dress. On the way home, Mama handed Jackie a brown paper bag.

"What is it, Mama?" she asked.

"Open it and see," Mama told her.

She closed her eyes and stuck one hand into the bag. As she pulled it out she opened her eyes. "Oh! It's the *HOME SWEET HOME* crocheted runner that I wanted. Thank you, Mama."

When the car stopped, Jackie jumped from the back seat and ran into the house. She returned with her Bible in her hand. She was on her way to read to Aunt Becky.

"Sit in the hammock beside me," Aunt Becky told her. "After you read the Bible, you can read some in *Ben-Hur*." She handed her the book.

Jackie opened her Bible to John 3:16 and began reading: *For God so loved the world, that he gave his only begotten Son, that whosoever believeth in him should not perish, but have everlasting life.*

Aunt Becky knew so much of her Bible from memory, that no matter which chapter Jackie chose to read from, Aunt Becky could say it right along with her.

When Jackie had read a chapter from *Ben-Hur*, Aunt Becky reached up and touched her head.

"You smell of outdoors," she said, "and I hear an excitement in your voice. Are you wanting to share it with me?"

Jackie looked into Aunt Becky's brown eyes that had so long ago been blinded by cataracts.

"Of course," Jackie told her. "Daddy took us to the Bodden Town Garden Party today. Did you ever go to a Garden Party, Aunt Becky?"

"Did I? Why yes, I went to many a one. My mother was from Bodden Town, you know."

"I didn't know that," Jackie told her. Then she saw the Garden Party out loud for Aunt Becky, and they laughed.

"The Plait Pole was a lot of fun," Jackie told her. "Did you ever plait it?"

"Yes, I did," she said, her eyes dancing. "Was ten years old. Saw Sam there that day. Ten years later I married him."

7

THE BELL RANG ONLY ONCE

"So creepy! Why would they bury someone inside the bell room?" Jackie asked.

"'Cause the story goes that she was already buried here when they built the church. And my mama says that it's not 'bell room,' it's 'belfry,'" Autumn told her.

"Well, whatever," Jackie said.

"In loving memory of…" Autumn continued.

"Time for the church bell to ring," Henry interrupted. "It's eleven o'clock," and then he left the room.

Jackie gasped. So exciting! The thick manila rope with the knot on the end dangled in front of her. She stared all the way up to the ceiling where a hole had been cut to let the rope through. *That rope must go all the way up to the very top of the church where the huge bell sits!* Jackie thought. She had seen the big boys and girls ring the bell many times.

But now she was the one standing beneath the rope. Children slid into her as they ran through the open door, hurrying to see who would ring the bell. The belfry was crowded now, making it hard for anyone to move.

Jackie held tightly to the big rope and pulled hard, and up, up, up she went…all the way to the ceiling. She heard only one *ding dong*, and then the bell stopped. What had she done wrong?

She tried to pull her arms up and down so the bell would ring, but the rope would not move, and her head was stuck to the top of the ceiling, and it hurt. *If only Mama had not put that big bow on top of my head!*

"Help, somebody help me!" she yelled. She looked for Autumn but she did not see her. She saw only a lot of laughing, scared children.

Jackie felt the room begin to spin—*such a strange feeling. She must be standing on her head!* Below her, she saw the children upside down. But mostly she saw the tops of their heads or their upturned faces with their mouths open.

"Get me down," she begged. "Somebody, go and get Henry. My hands hurt."

Jackie knew that she would not be able to hold on much longer, but she was afraid to let go of the rope. It looked so-o-o-o-o far down to the floor. And anyway, she could not see the floor. She knew that if she fell, she would fall on children.

She closed her eyes and began to pray. "Dear Jesus, please help me to get down from here," she prayed. "I will try to remember to never pull this rope again. Thanks. Jackie."

There was confusion below now. Henry was pushing everyone aside with his hands.

"Let me through," he said. "Stay away from the ladder."

Henry's feet pounded on the steps as he almost ran up the ladder. Then Jackie could hear them no more.

Just as she thought she could hold onto the rope no longer, she felt her head leave the ceiling. Slowly the rope moved down, down, down. The children scattered. Some laughed, some gasped as she was lowered to the ground.

"Thank you, Jesus," Jackie said silently.

Just as they began filing through the side door to go into church, she heard heavy footsteps coming down the ladder.

"Wait right there, children," Henry said. "This is not funny. The rope on the bell was all tangled. Did you see what could happen to any one of you?"

"Yes." It was almost a whisper.

"Then, unless you're old enough and big enough, don't try to ring the bell!" He turned to Jackie and said, "Are you okay?" She nodded.

Before going into the north wing of the church, Jackie smoothed her soft dress and rubbed her tired hands together. Then she slipped quietly into the long pew beside Jane.

The clock above the pulpit read 11:07. The bell had rung only once, but the grownups were all in church as if nothing had happened.

All across the church she saw her friends slip into benches and sit in their usual places. Daddy looked at Mama and raised his eyebrows. Mama shrugged her shoulders.

The congregation stood and sang:
Little children, little children, who love their Redeemer
Are the jewels, precious jewels,

His loved and His own.
Like the stars of the morning,
His bright crown adorning,
They shall shine in their beauty,
Bright gems for His crown.

Jackie felt like a gem or a jewel. Jesus loved her enough to answer her prayer. She was special!

When Church was over and they were at last in the back seat of Daddy's car, Jane fumbled with Jackie's ribbon bow.

"What did you do to this bow?" she asked

"Nothing," Jackie said.

"Nothing! Well it's all smashed flat with your head. Something must have happened."

"I was praying," Jackie told her.

"Praying? On your head?"

"It was the bestest prayer I ever said. And I said it on my head!"

8

A DOVE NAMED HIPPITY HOP

"They're back," Jackie told Baw Baw, pointing to the flock of ground doves pecking in the sand in the back yard.

"So what?" Baw Baw asked.

"Well, my dove named Hop Hop is not here again. I hope nothing has happened to him."

"Is that all you got to worry about? One ground dove?"

Jackie's eyes searched among the birds as they fought over the bits of scratch feed that Daddy had thrown out for the chickens.

Old Smokey, the stray cat, strutted around in a stiff-legged fashion in an effort to drive the doves off, but they seemed not to see him.

Finally, Jackie went back to the #2 washtub beneath the breadfruit tree with its scrub-board and bar of brown soap. She was washing her school uniforms. After she had hung them on the line, she picked up her canvas shoes and washed them until they were sparkling white. Then she poured the water out, rinsed the tub, and leaned it against the root of the tree.

She was about to go inside the house and lay out her clothes for church the next day when Washerwoman rounded the corner.

"I come to wash the baby's clothes," she said.

"Okay, I'll go and tell Mama you're here."

Just as Jackie returned with the baby's clothes, Baw Baw stuck her head out the kitchen window. "Be sure you leave those nappies in the boiling water for twenty minutes to sterilize them," she said. "That's what Nurse Donna ordered when she was here."

"Yes, ma'am," Washerwoman told her.

Mr. Konrad arrived and laid a piece of wood across the wood horse and began sawing it.

"How you do today?" Washerwoman asked him.

Baw Baw answered, "He's got no time to talk. He's late getting here, and I need that wood right now for the stove." Then she grabbed a machete and dug in the dirt just at the edge of the crawl space beneath the kitchen. She felt around in the sand and pulled out a big cassava root and a yam.

"Who would have thought they would grow under there?" Jackie asked.

"Don't they teach you anything in school? They didn't grow there, I buried them to keep them fresh until it was time to cook them."

"Oh!" Jackie said.

"What you cooking for Sunday dinner?" Washerwoman asked.

"That chicken right there in the fowl coop. She's been in there three weeks eating only chicken feed. Should be clean enough for Sunday dinner now."

Mr. Konrad didn't say a word. He just sawed the wood and stacked it in a pile, and Baw Baw took an armload to the kitchen and the firewood crackled in the wood-burning stove.

Jackie sat beneath the sweetsop tree and strung the laces in her white canvas shoes before pinning them to the line to dry.

"Guess what, Washerwoman?" she asked.

"What?"

"I went to the Bodden Town Garden Party and it was fun. Have you ever seen them dance the quadrille?"

"Have I?" she replied.

Suddenly her feet began to jig, dust stirred and Mr. Konrad played a tune with his saw. Jackie stood and danced the quadrille the way she had seen them dance it, but Washerwoman's feet moved much faster than hers.

Baw Baw's mouth was in a pout. "Unny stop this foolishness," she said. "Ain't no time for all this on a Saturday morning."

But the music continued and the dust rose and the chicken squawked in the coop and mockingbirds sang in the banana trees and Daddy strolled by.

"Hotdog!" he said. "This looks like Grand Central Station!"

"Whatever that is," Washerwoman laughed.

Daddy threw more cracked corn out and the doves covered the ground. The dancing stopped and Jackie searched once more for Hop Hop. Then, she saw him and beside him a tiny bird fought for the food he fed him. Jackie sprang among them and tried to catch Hop Hop, but they all flew away.

Daddy was almost to the printing shop, but he spun around and saw what she had done.

"What do you think you're doing?" he asked.

Jackie walked toward him. "I'm going to catch Hop Hop for my very own pet, Daddy. I'll take good care of him and keep him in a cage because he can't run as fast as the others with that short leg."

"You'll do no such thing," Daddy said. "He deserves to be free. He would rather live one day in the wild than his whole life protected in a cage."

"But he's mine, Daddy. I named him."

"No, he's not. And you don't even have the name right. It's not Hop Hop. It should be Hippity Hop. Didn't you see there was a baby bird beside her?"

Jackie began to cry, but Daddy put an arm around her shoulder, "Do you see Washerwoman yonder? Would you cage her to protect her?" he asked.

"No, Daddy."

"Well, one of her legs is shorter than the other, but did you see how happy she was as she danced? That's because her mother allowed her to be free."

"Thank you, Daddy, now I understand," Jackie said. "Hippity Hop must go free."

9

A CAYMAN COWBOY

Jackie sat on a high limb of the plum tree eating juicy red plums and counting cricket skeletons that were fastened to the branches. From her perch in the plum tree, she heard a voice say, "Come to mama, please come to mama!" In the distance she saw Ms. Maud kneeling beside the well in the yard next door, one hand reaching far down inside it.

Jackie hurried down the tree and ran toward the kitchen door.

"Baw Baw, please may I have the dipper with the long rope?"

"Don't be silly," Baw Baw said. "You know 1 don't give you no dipper. Run along and play."

"But Baw Baw, Ms. Maud's kitten fell into Lindy's well and she can't get it out."

Baw Baw peered out the kitchen window. "I declare, there's always something going on," she said. Then she hurried toward the dipper. "Here, but bring it back when you're done with it, and wash it!"

"Where are you going?" Washerwoman called, her hands clinging to the clothesline.

"To get a kitten out of the well," Jackie told her.

When she was finally beside the well, she saw Ms. Maud dangling over the side, one arm beckoning to the cat to catch hold of it. Deep down in the well, a kitten's claws held fast to the rocky side. His wet fur clung to him and he trembled like a leaf in the wind. A tiny meow echoed in the well.

Ms. Maud lifted her tearstained face to Jackie and said, "It's my cat, you know. He's my baby, my kitten!"

"It's okay," Jackie told her. "I'll help you get him out." She lowered the dipper into the well and Ms. Maud moaned, "Jump in the bucket baby, come to mama!" But the kitten did not move.

While the rescue continued, a lonely cowboy song could be heard in the distance. As the voice grew nearer, a young boy wearing a cowboy shirt and hat came into view. His dusty feet galloped along as he rode his stick horse. Strapped around him, his holster and guns glared in the morning sunlight.

"Will you get my cat out of the well?" Ms. Maud asked him.

"Okay, on my way back," he told her. "I'll help on my way back. Mama needs flour and sugar."

As he rounded the corner on his way to Daddy's store, his guitar hung loosely around his shoulders and his song trailed behind him:

Nobody's business, nobody's business,
Nobody's business but my own!

Ms. Maud sat beneath the star-apple tree now, fanning herself with her apron, still singing her own little song:

Cat in the well! Oh, I say, cat in the well!

"I think I'll go and wait on the corner for the cowboy," she told them. "He's little enough to lower into the well and rescue my baby."

Washerwoman arrived, drying her hands on her frock skirt.

"Let me try," she said. Jackie was glad to hand her the rope and move back because green frogs with bulging eyes and smiles on their faces jumped everywhere.

When Washerwoman had wrapped the rope around her hand a couple of times, she lowered the dipper below the kitten. As she moved her hand back and forth she sang:

And the little cow-cow, and the little bow-wow,
And the wee-wee cat.
And the little kitty cat says, meow, meow, meow,
And the cow-cow says, moo-moo,
And the little doggie says, ruff-ruff, ruff-ruff.

She had no sooner barked like a dog than they heard a scratching sound against the bucket.

"My-oh-my!" Washerwoman said. "I scared him right into the dipper." As she began pulling the cat up, Jackie saw the cowboy come around the corner. He held on to two small brown paper bags as he galloped down the dirt path toward home.

Ms. Maud trailed behind him, "Catch him," she called. "Somebody catch him. Let's lower him down into the well."

But the Cayman Cowboy zipped by, a smile on his face, a paradise plum candy in plain view in the side of his jaw.

Washerwoman inched the dipper up the side of the well and the cowboy never turned his head. His guitar hung lopsided on his back and the song began once more,

> *I'm minding nobody's business,*
> *Nobody's business,*
> *Nobody's business but my own.*

10

SKINNY-LEE-LEE

"Let's go to Mr. Dan's shop and buy a chocolate candy," Jackie told Kerrie Sue. "There's still time to eat it before the school bell rings."

The two friends put their money together and counted it and giggled as they passed the Town Hall. School children wandered aimlessly around it whispering, others trying to peep into the open windows.

When the girls had walked the short distance and shared the melting chocolate candy bar, they strolled back toward school, licking the chocolate from the candy wrapper.

Ken was climbing one of the pillars that surrounded the Town Hall, peeping in through the open window. Friends pushed him upward and held on to his legs in an effort to keep him from falling.

"Goodness, I wonder what is going on in Grand Court today? Must be something good, or there wouldn't be so many people around here." Jackie said.

"Skinny-Lee-Lee!" Ken yelled, "Skinny-Lee-Lee is on the witness stand!" Then he jumped down and called out, "Run, everybody, she's coming after us."

Boys and girls scattered from around the building. Some fell and cried, stopping long enough to wipe sand and gravel and blood from sore knees.

A tiny wisp of a woman darted through the front door, waving a knobby stick high in the air. Then she spun around and yelled back, "See, Judge, see what I tell ya. The children not got no manners."

A policeman stopped her, but she slid away from him and ran after the children, throwing her stick through the air.

"Unny cockroaches," she screamed. "Unny mothers don't teach you no manners. Unny fathers don't teach you no manners. Unny teachers don't teach you no manners. I gonna teach you manners." She bent forward, her eyes scanning the ground, and she tossed a rock among the children.

Jackie and Kerrie Sue were safe inside the schoolyard, but some of their friends still ran aimlessly in the street, trying to find a hiding place from Ms. Dulcianna.

She was almost to the schoolyard when the cry echoed through the air again, "Skinny-Lee-Lee!" Her long skirt scraped the ground as she spun around and headed toward the big Town Clock that sat in front of the Town Hall. Ken and three of his friends were hiding behind it.

She picked up her stick from the road and flung it at them only moments after they had taken shelter behind the big guinep tree beside the public library.

Mr. John Bolton stirred in sleep, his head hanging over the cement ledge surrounding the library. Lizards with long tails and ballooned throats shared the ledge with him.

The boys laughed and whispered and hid behind the tree, just a short distance from where he lay.

"What's going on? Eh? Eh?" he asked the boys, shaking his head and opening one eye.

"Hush!" Ken whispered, one finger against his lips.

Ms. Dulcianna hurried toward the guinep tree, her thick black wig dangling sideways on her head, rocks still flying through the air. A swarm of mosquitoes followed behind her, singing their buzzing tune. Arms waved in the air and she slapped at them in an effort to drive them away.

"Oh, Skinny-Lee-Lee, eh?" Mr. John Bolton said, a crooked smile on his face. Only moments later a rock zipped past his head and hit the library.

"Ms. Dulcianna!" a stern voice said. "Someone is going to get hurt!" It was Mr. Trent, hurrying toward the gate.

She spun around and fixed her little beady eyes on him for a moment. A rock slid from her hand and she reached up and straightened her wig.

As she staggered toward Mr. Trent, she rolled her eyes and stuck out her tongue.

"Your school young-uns ain't got no manners," She told him. "No manners at all. They don't need no learning. They need manners."

"Have they been bothering you?" Mr. Trent asked.

"Bothering me? Why yes. They're nuisances. Pests. Got no manners. None at all," she told him. "Don't know how to treat a lady like me! Here I am explaining my complaint to the Court, and they calling me names through the window."

"I'm sorry, Ms. Dulcianna," Mr. Trent said. "I can assure you they will be justly punished."

"Well, I trust you to do just that," she told him. "Now, if you'll excuse me, I must get back in Court. The Judge is waiting for me there!"

11

REMEMBRANCE DAY THROUGH A CHILD'S EYES

Jackie stood between Jane and Judy around the Memorial Cross in the Presbyterian church yard. On the other side of Jane, Daddy grasped John's hand, his white knuckles revealing how tightly he held onto the child. *Almost as if he were afraid to let go of him,* Jackie thought. Beside John, baby Joy slept in Mama's arms.

A cool northwest breeze swept in from over the sea, causing Jackie's thin cotton dress to cling to her. Fluttering on her shoulder, a red poppy on a lone wire struggled to be free, held in place only by a safety pin. But she must not let it fly away, so she covered it with her hand.

The crowd grew as the congregation surrounded the cross, a whole sea of people, all dressed in white, wearing poppies on their shoulders and solemn faces. Jackie had forgotten how touching a Remembrance Day service could be. It seemed to her that everyone's gaze was fixed only on the cross.

At 10:30 the wind carried the usual Remembrance Day hymn:

O God, our help in ages past
Our hope for years to come,
Our shelter from the stormy blast,
And our eternal home.
Time like an ever-rolling stream
Bears all its sons away,
They fly forgotten as a dream
Dies at the opening day.
O God our help in ages past,
Our hope for years to come,
Be thou our guard while life shall last,
And our eternal home.

The Commissioner of the Island stepped forward and made a speech honouring the men who fought in all the wars. Women wiped their eyes with their handkerchiefs, and men stood, hands behind them, tight lines around their lips. Jackie's legs trembled, from what she did not know, as the cool wind made a mournful sound whipping through the nearby almond trees.

"They shall not grow old," a lady said, and others joined her:

They shall not grow old as we that are left grow old,
Age shall not weary nor the years condemn,
At the going down of the sun and in the morning
We will remember them.

The Chief of Police, standing at attention, straight and tall in full uniform, studied his watch. At exactly 11:00 all heads bowed and one minute of silence in honour of the dead was observed.

When the minute of silence was over, the Commissioner stepped forward and laid a wreath of poppies

on the Memorial Cross. Then he saluted. The Chief of Police also laid a wreath on the cross and saluted, and still others followed him until many wreaths had been laid.

Jackie tried to think of other things. She remembered how fast her legs pedaled her bicycle a few days earlier as she went from house to house selling poppies. She sold them every year because she knew that the money made from selling them went to the veterans' fund. And they were easy to sell. The adults all bought double-layer petals while the children bought single-layer poppies. She looked around for Ms. Jane Pic-Pic. She had taught her a few lines of a poem the day she sold her one, and Jackie tried to recall the words now:

> *On Flanders Field the poppies grow*
> *Beside the crosses, row by row,*
> *That mark the graves...*

But Ms. Jane Pic-Pic was nowhere in sight to help her remember the rest.

A parade marched on the road in front of the Church, and the Commissioner took a salute. Boy Scouts and Cubs carrying colourful flags marched by, followed by the Girls' Guild, all in uniform. The Chief of Police marched by, followed by the police and their band, and just behind them, the veterans came into view.

It was all so solemn, all so beautiful, all so hard for a little girl not yet twelve to understand.

When finally Jackie was home and dinner was over, she sneaked into the hammock beside Mama.

"Tell me, Mama, did you ever know anyone who died in the war?" Jackie asked her.

"Yes, I did, I knew many people," Mama told her, brushing the damp hair back from the small face.

"Can you tell me about one, Mama? It's so hard to seem real if you don't know someone."

"I can tell you about my Uncle Vernon."

"Okay, Mama."

"Well, when I was just a girl like you, I often saw my Granny rocking in a rocking chair and wiping her eyes. I knew she was crying for her young son who had died in the war. As she rocked she repeated:

I didn't raise my boy to be a soldier.
I brought him up to be my pride and joy.
Who dared to place a musket on his shoulder
To fight some other mother's darling boy?
There'd be no war today, if mothers all would say,
"I didn't raise my boy to be a soldier."

"I hate wars, Mama! I hate the enemies that fight us!"

"Wait a minute now, child. Hate is too big a word for you. Remember, my Granny was not only heartbroken because her son was a soldier. She was also heartbroken because he had been trained to fight some other mother's darling boy."

"I see, Mama. War hurts both sides, doesn't it?"

"Yes, it does, darling," Mama said hugging her. "I want you to always remember that enemies have bodies and a heart. Enemies are people!"

12

COWBOYS AND INDIANS

Jackie played a game of jacks with Missy, Jane, Rita, and Judy.

"Go and get us the jacks from the crawl space beneath the floor where they fell through the crack," Judy told her.

"Why do I always have to be the one to go and get them?" Jackie asked.

"Because you're the smallest, and it's easy for you to crawl there and get them."

"Not so!" Jackie told her. "I'm taller than you and you know it."

"But you're younger, so that does it," Judy said.

Jackie's feelings were hurt, but she did not let them know. She did what they asked and handed them the dusty jacks.

"Your turn," Jane said.

"I'm not playing anymore," Jackie told them.

"Oh, she's insulted," Jane said. "Acting just like Uncle Bill."

That did it. She left the room in tears, though she never let them see. She would go and play with her friends April and Kim.

Ahead of her lay a shortcut straight through Cousin Melinda's yard, but Jackie was afraid of Cousin Melinda's husband, Mr. Bugger.

While she stood outside his gate, half hidden behind an oleander tree, she saw him, sitting on the floor of his one-room house, the windows and doors wide open. In his hand was a piece of thatch straw and he was picking sand from between the seams of the unpainted wood floor.

Through the kitchen window, Jackie waved to Cousin Melinda as she fanned the fire in her caboose. She put a finger over her mouth, and Jackie sneaked quietly across the newly swept sandyard. She had made it past the house when a stick flew through the air, barely missing her.

"Get out of my yard," he yelled. "Look at your big ugly footprints, messing up my yard."

Jackie ran real fast until she stood in front of April and Kim's house. But Mr. Bugger held on to the fence between the two yards, swaying back and forth. His top lip was rolled back much like a biting dog, showing his scant teeth in front.

"Next time I'll catch you," he said. "I won't miss."

Jackie was still shaken, but April handed her a ripe naseberry, and Kim joined them, and the three friends sat under the naseberry tree eating sweet brown naseberries and spitting the flat black seeds on the ground.

Tim, Brian, and Matt came by, their stick guns stuck in their pockets. They talked and laughed awhile, and Brian asked, "Want to play cowboys and Indians?"

The girls whispered to each other, then said, "Okay, we'll play cowboys and Indians if you will first watch our concert. It's a good one. We've been practicing it for weeks."

"Oh, gee," Brian said, flailing his arms in the air. "I don't think so."

"We'll serve refreshments," Jackie told them. "Swanky, made from Mama's Seville oranges and brown sugar along with hard tacks and guava jam."

"Well, maybe," he said. "What do you think, guys?"

"Okay," they said.

The girls pulled out the bottle of swanky that had been made days earlier, when they had tried to get the sisters to watch their concert.

"It's kind of old," Kim whispered.

"They'll never know," Jackie told her.

They poured the swanky in tin cups that belonged in the little house under the tangerine tree, and the fellows sipped it as they sat on the ground beneath the big guinep tree.

April, Kim and Jackie smoothed their dresses and brushed their hair back and smiled. Jackie stepped forward, "Today, I'll recite Winken, Blinken, and Nod."

Brian punched Matt and laughed, "Matt, ole boy, you sure you want to stay and hear this? We could be fishing."

Matt grunted and Jackie told him, "Be quiet and listen," then she began:

The owl and the pussycat went to sea
In a beautiful pea-green boat
They took some money and plenty of honey
Wrapped up in a five-pound note.
"Where are you going and what do you wish?"
The old moon asked the three.

*"We're out to fish for herring fish
That live in the deep blue sea.
Nets of silver and gold have we,"
Said Winken, Blinken, and Nod.*

Jackie smiled and curtsied and walked to the other end of the porch.

"How stupid!" Brian murmured to his friends. "She took two verses from two different poems and said them together. "Winken, Blinken, and Nod ain't the same poem as The Owl and the Pussycat."

"Well, it sounded good," Jackie told them. But they laughed even harder.

"That's it," Tim said. "No more reciting. It's our turn to play cowboys and Indians."

The girls took their stand behind the porch posts and the boys had the whole front yard.

"We know who's going to win," Tim said. "Right, Matt?" He just smiled and nodded.

Bang-bang, roared the shooting from behind the swing in the front yard. *Bang, bang, bang,* and Brian ran toward the naseberry tree. But just before he made it to shelter, there was a loud *pow* and he was shot. He flung his stick gun high in the air, and kicked it when it fell.

"Good job, Kim. One down and two to go," April said.

Jackie slipped from one post to another trying to get Tim as he scrounged for falling guineps. *Pow, pow,* but he got away.

Just then a peculiar noise roared down the dirt path on the opposite side of April's yard.

A wheelbarrow carrying blind Uncle Bill to visit his friend whisked by, with him singing:

Wedding bells are ringing in the chapel
That should be ringing now for you and me.
Down the aisle with someone else you're walking.
Those wedding bells will never ring for me.

Just then the wheelbarrow tipped, and chubby Uncle Bill rolled out.

Tim and Matt laughed and ran to try and help him up, but two shots rang through the air. *Pow, pow.* The last two cowboys were dead.

"That wasn't fair," Brian yelled. "We need to call it quits and start over."

"Okay," Jackie said. "But first you'll have to watch our concert. This time April will recite for you *"Will you walk into my parlour," said the spider to the fly.*

"Oh, no!" Brian growled, a scowl on his face. "On second thought, maybe you girls did win fair and square after all. Let's go, guys!"

13

SHIP AHOY!

"Ship ahoy!" sounded the cry from far in the distance. Jackie and April's game of marbles halted.

"Gotta go!" Jackie said and she ran as fast as she could. By the time she reached the shore in back of Daddy's store, a crowd had gathered. Far in the distance a ship, resembling a toy on the horizon, sailed toward the shore.

Baw Baw stood beneath the big sea grape tree, rubbing her hands together and smiling. "Ship ahoy, ship ahoy," she chanted, and beckoned toward the dirt road for friends to join her.

From far inland Islanders came, some holding tiny children by the hand, some with babies in their arms, some laughing, others crying.

"I wish it would anchor in the harbour," Jane said. "Wouldn't that be something to remember?"

"I saw many a one anchor in my lifetime," Baw Baw chimed in.

Grapes lay beneath the tree and the south breeze brought with it the sweet smell of ripe fruit.

Jackie reached up and picked a sea grape leaf, rolled it in the shape of a cone and began filling it with fat juicy grapes. She knew she must pick up as many as she could, because soon they would all be trampled. She plopped a sweet, dusty one in her mouth.

Rita and Judy sat on a huge rock in Papa's bay trading marbles, their feet dangling in the rippling water.

"Clear the way," Rita yelled, pointing toward a side road.

From down Mr. Ralph's road came a truck, backfiring and puffing out smoke as it rolled along. It crossed over the marl road and parked on the shore side, a short distance from the store.

Honk-honk, cried the old truck's horn. Children clapped their hands and waved to the rickety truck.

A sailboat headed out to the harbour, leaving a thin trail of foam behind it. Catboats cut through the calm water, the men rowing feverishly as they headed toward the huge ship.

Across from Jackie, under the popnut tree. Daddy waved his handkerchief. Then, he walked out to the farthest point of the shore. He stood there all by himself for a long time, his pipe in his mouth, his white cap waving back and forth in his hand.

"In just a short time, the boat will reach the big ship," Jane said. "I hope Caymanians are on it."

Stretching across the marl road, cars lined the shore. They blew their horns and blinked their lights, welcoming the ship.

The ship's whistle screamed louder and louder. *Such a sad sound,* Jackie thought. People around her spoke almost in whispers.

Just as the sailboat approached the ship, it turned around and smoke trailed from the smokestack. It was headed out of the harbour.

One fisherman threw one of his paddles in the air in disgust and used the second one to retrieve it. Other boats came toward shore.

With the setting of the sun, the crowd dwindled one by one. Adults headed toward home, their eyes downcast, their shoulders slumped, while children frolicked beside them, unaware of the disappointment the grown-ups felt at not having a loved one come ashore.

When Jackie's family gathered in the living room that night for worship. Daddy put his hand on his forehead, his fingers almost covering his eyes. He cleared his throat. "There were Caymanians on that boat today," he said. "Somebody's husband, brother, or son!"

He chose a hymn in honour of the seamen, and they sang:

Brightly beams our Father's mercy
From His lighthouse evermore;
But to us He gives the keeping
Of the lights along the shore.
Let the lower lights be burning!
Send the gleam across the wave!
Some poor fainting, struggling seaman
You may rescue, you may save.

After each family member had taken a turn reading from a chapter in the Bible, Daddy prayed for the Cayman seamen on that ship, ending with the Lord's Prayer.

Several weeks passed, and one day Jackie rode her bicycle to the George Town post office, the mailbox key in her hand. As she rounded the corner by the big Town Clock, she saw the crowd. People walked quickly toward the post office, greeting each other.

Soon she leaned her bicycle against the post office colonnade, and walked inside, twining her way between adults and children.

"Theresa Shroyer," Henry called out. "Anyone here for Theresa Shroyer?"

"I'll take it to her," Ms. Dova said, and she reached her hand up for the letter.

"Next!" Henry continued. "Bart Matthews."

"Here," he replied, and the letter moved from hand to hand until it reached Mr. Bart in the back of the crowd.

By that time, Jackie had arrived at her letterbox. She turned the key and pulled out an airmail envelope all edged in blue and red. The wheels on her bicycle made a hissing sound as she hurried toward home.

When Daddy had read the letter, he walked from the printing shop to the house and handed it to Mama.

"You'll never guess what it says," Daddy told her.

"Tell me," Mama said. "I'm too curious to have to wait and read it."

"Buddy was on that ship that came into the harbour a couple of weeks ago. They were passing by the Island and though the ship's schedule was tight time-wise, its

Captain pulled in long enough for my brother to see the old homestead."

"I declare," Mama said. "So close and yet not close enough!"

"Looking through binoculars, he said he saw the house and the gray store across the street from it," Daddy told her, "and out on the very point of the shore, he saw someone dressed in white, waving to them."

14

TWO CAYMAN BROTHERS REMEMBER

In my second book, By the Seashore of Cayman, *I told the story entitled "A Pirate's Treasure". Shortly after the book was released, I received a call from Carlston, a friend that I had grown up with. He was laughing and told me that he had just read the chapter that I mentioned above, and he wanted to tell me the rest of the story.*

"I was nine and my brother Mervin was six," Carlston said. "My uncle had just returned from his travels abroad. We all gathered around to listen to the stories he told of the places he had been. It was then that he produced an oatmeal box full of coins from his travels, most of them being American coins."

"That's enough now, boys, go out and play," their mother told them. They drew a circle and a game of marbles had begun when they heard shots ring through the air, and they ran back inside the house. His uncle had a gun in his hand, the bullets riddling the oatmeal box that had held the strange money. Coins flew in every direction, covering the ground beneath it. Finally the bullets stopped and the boys scooped up hands full of the strange coins. They filled their pockets, and Mervin found an empty talcum powder can, filled it, and replaced the lid.

Carlston took his money to Daddy's store and bought a can of corned beef with some of his coins. By the time he arrived home, he heard his mother's voice. "Boys, you can't keep that money," she said. "Give every cent of it back to your uncle." But it was too late. Mervin had already buried his talcum powder can filled with coins, and Carlston had spent some of his in Daddy's store. However, they emptied their pockets of the remaining coins and returned them to their uncle.

Mervin left some of his treasure in savings, buried in God's good earth, and for a long while the two brothers put the incident our of their minds.

When finally they recalled their precious childhood treasure, Mervin could no longer remember where he had buried it. They searched in all their favourite hiding places and dug beneath the beloved trees of youth, but the talcum powder can was nowhere in sight.

Years passed and the boys became men and often many stories of their childhood were rehashed. One of the best loved remained the story of the lost treasure. Finally, a few short years before my book was written, they made a decision.

"Carlston, on your next visit home I want you to bring a metal detector," Mervin said. "Then we can scan every parcel of ground that we played on. Wouldn't that be fun?"

Before the detector was bought and the next visit arrived, my book was released and fell into Carlston's hands.

"I called Mervin after I had read A Pirate's Treasure," *Carlston continued, "And I told him to forget about the metal detector because Jackie had found his lost coins*

many years ago beneath the huge rock a short distance from her daddy's store."

"We laughed so hard that neither of us could talk for several minutes," Carlston said. "Finally Mervin asked, '*Well tell me, what did she spend it on?*'"

"Dunno," Carlston said, "But I'm real thankful that the mystery of your lost coins has finally been solved."

15

A SUNDAY EVENING WALK

Autumn stepped from her porch just as Anna and Jackie rounded the corner. "Want to go for a Sunday evening walk with us?" Anna asked.

"Yes, I've been hoping you would come by," Autumn said. Then she turned and waved to her mother, who was rocking in the swing.

The three girls held hands and spread across the road, swinging their arms.

"Look, they've begun clearing the land for the movie theatre they're going to build," Anna said. "I wonder what movies will look like."

"Well, we'll know soon enough," Autumn told her.

"Right now, I'd settle for a ride on that merry-go-round over there. Isn't it lovely?" Jackie said pointing off to the left. "Look, the horses are all smiling." Little children played all around it, some climbing on the horses. Jackie wished that the music would begin and the horses would move, but of course, they didn't on a Sunday.

Farther down, they saw the big cotton tree standing tall just beyond Dobson Hall.

Suddenly Anna moved to the seaside of the road. "See, here is the mark where the Home Guard soldier fell and hit the root of the tree!" The three girls peered down at the big root that protruded from the ground. Jackie remembered well the Sunday that he had fallen.

"Mama said it is only God's mercy that he is still alive and healthy," Autumn continued. She moved toward the wooden steps that had been nailed to the tree as a ladder for the men to climb on.

"Nobody other than the soldiers has ever been brave enough to climb it," Anna said.

"You mean the soldiers and the men who built the lookout house at the very top of the tree!" Autumn corrected her.

"Well, yes," Anna agreed. "My cousin Howard said that when he was in the lookout house, he could see across the whole Island. He said no enemy ships could get near without the Home Guard soldiers seeing them through the spyglass."

But the war was over now, and the little peek-a-boo windows in the lookout house were closed. Jackie knew that the cotton tree was much higher than the big almond tree that had fallen during the storm.

Anna was walking around the broken wall of the old George Town Fort that surrounded the cotton tree, sticking her hands through the small lookout holes in the fort and laughing.

"You're going to ruin your pretty dress," Autumn told her, stepping over the black cannon in the middle of the fort.

The three girls waved to Ted and his brothers as they sat on the upstairs porch of the stately home across from the fort. Another cotton tree shaded that house, although it was not near so high as the big cotton tree with the lookout house.

Ted pointed toward the garage, alerting Jackie that Daddy's car was there, waiting to be worked on. Jackie smiled and nodded. Beyond the garage, the three girls giggled and sang:

Mr. Kelly is a good old man,
He tries to teach us all he can,
Reading, writing and 'rithmetic,
And he never forgets to whip with his stick.

They chanted the song over and over until the one-room schoolhouse on stilts with its many windows was behind them. They had learned the song from some of their friends who attended that school.

"It's hard to believe that Daddy went to school in that building," Jackie muttered partly to herself.

"Our grandfathers might have even gone there," Autumn added. But soon it was behind them.

"Want to ring the church bell again?" Anna teased as they passed the Presbyterian church where all three girls attended Sunday school.

"Never!" Jackie told her.

The warehouse and dock lay before them off to the right. The dock was empty now, but Jackie remembered a time when there were rows and rows of turtles on their backs waiting to be sold. She wondered if they'd had tears in their eyes. *But she must not think about that now!*

Friends rode past on bicycles, ringing bells and waving. Soon they approached the stores in George Town. The white wooden buildings all lined in a row were closed and the streets mostly deserted.

Children playfully splashed them with water as they passed Hog Sty Bay.

Jackie pointed to a dark area off the shore. "I bet that's Eden Rock," she said.

"How would you know?" Anna asked.

"'Cause I went around it in a canoe once."

"Take me next time," Anna told her. "I want to see it too."

They turned into Ms. Nell's yard and knocked on her door. She met them outside with her camera. When they had posed around a willow tree, she snapped their picture.

"They'll be ready in a week," she told them. "Stop by next Sunday evening."

Anna was ready to turn back, but the others wanted to go further.

"We're almost there," Autumn told her. "See, there's the trawlers where they build the vessels."

Sprawled before them, Jackie saw the biggest, prettiest vessel she had ever seen. It rested in a well-shaded spot beneath almond trees.

She climbed the platform beside it so that she could see the inside.

"You better get down from there before you rip your dress," Anna said.

But Jackie wasn't worried about her dress. She wanted to see the big steering wheel and touch the dark smooth wood around it. She was dreaming of faraway places that it might travel to and wondering if children would play on its deck.

In the midst of her daydream, she glanced up to see Anna and Autumn far down the road. She hurried and caught up with them, only to make a stop at Petra Plantation, where they sipped lemonade as Ms. Helga told them all about the people who would sail on the big vessel.

16

A SCHOONER IS LAUNCHED

"Pull!" Captain Bodden called to the men holding the huge ropes. "Pull men, pull!"

"Hurrah!" shouted the crowd, and the band struck up a tune. Mr. Brady played his fiddle and the men pulling the ropes sang:

> *Oh, Miss Lucianna,*
> *There are rocky high mountains*
> *You cannot climb over...*

"Let's move it! All hands on the rope! Now, p-u-l-l!"

"Oh!" the women gasped, wiping their eyes with their lace handkerchiefs as the yacht moved the first few inches.

Children held hands and danced in a circle in the shade of the almond trees that grew at the very edge of South Sound. Beneath dresses of lace and ribbons, their can-can slips twirled.

"There she goes!" Captain Bodden yelled. "Let's keep her going." And the magnificent boat crept along on rollers made from thatch palm tree trunks.

Under the shade of the almond trees, women set up long tables and covered them with cloths. They moved ever so carefully so as not to ruin their lovely dresses. They brought the food that they had prepared a day earlier and placed it on the tables and covered it.

"Stop!" Captain Bodden shouted. "No more pulling. The rollers are slipping and the boat is tilting."

A gasp went up almost like a whisper among the crowd. The band stopped playing. Women halted. Children became quiet. No one danced, except Sally. She twirled in the middle of the street, a red hibiscus flower in the side of her gray hair. She laughed her cute little toothless smile, unaware that the canvas shoes on her dancing toes were on the wrong feet.

"Move the logs. While you're at it, bring the ones from the back and put them in front so we won't have to stop to do that later," Captain Bodden said.

Men hurried now, doing as they were told, ignoring the sweat that dripped from the tips of their noses.

"Now pull from the right side and let's straighten her up!" he told them.

"Hurrah," cried the crowd as the boat straightened and began to roll ever so slowly toward the sea.

Women relaxed now, sitting on low limbs of trees, fanning with accordion fans decorated with oriental girls. They conversed with friends from all over the Island. Some took off their hats and fanned with them.

Every so often Jackie ran over to Mama and took baby sister, Joy, from her so that she could rest.

Jackie knew that Joy liked her little friend, Lerita, so she spread a baby blanket and set the two on it to play. They shared rattles and squeeze toys and stuffed animals and pulled at the camphor that had been tied in a piece of cloth and pinned to their dresses. Mama said it was to ward off colds.

"Such pretty babies," a passerby remarked.

"Roll," went up the call. "Let it roll! Let's get it a bit further, then we'll break for lunch and get out of the sun."

High in the almond trees, parrots jabbered and cut green almonds from the branches, dropping them like rain to the ground.

Women stopped talking and lifted the cloth cover from the food. Clustered on the far corner of the table sat the turtle stew and beef that had been slaughtered a day earlier, conch stew in coconut gravy and sea pie and crabs baked in their own backs. Fried ripe plantain, steamed yam, sweet potato, breadfruit, rice, and macaroni and cheese covered the center of the table. The desserts were on the other end. There was cassava cake, yam cake, yellow cake with fresh grated coconut icing, and jelly rolls.

The Commissioner's car rolled to a stop and the band played the National Anthem. The Union Jack waved in the breeze on the front of his car, and when the door was opened, the new Commissioner and his wife stepped out. The cheering crowd welcomed them and little Maria presented the First Lady with a bouquet of flowers. Then she took her place with her husband at the head of the table.

Tired men left the ropes and moved forward in a straight line, wiping their faces with handkerchiefs. Jackie wondered how the food would stretch to feed all these many people from all over the Island. But when the men had been served, the ladies helped the childrens' plates, and they sat on the ground in the shade of the trees and ate.

As the huge platters and bowls became empty, the women trekked back and forth to the cars, bringing more food. When everyone had been fed, there was food left over.

Mr. Phil played the mouth organ and Lerita's dad, Mr. Harley, danced with Lerita in his arms. She giggled as he sang:

> *Beautiful, beautiful brown eyes,*
> *Beautiful, beautiful brown eyes,*
> *Beautiful, beautiful brown eyes,*
> *I'll never love blue eyes again.*

A short distance away, Daddy sat on a low grape tree limb and bounced Joy on his knee and sang:

> *Oh, the sweetest girl in this world*
> *Is my Kookie-Nannie.*
> *Yes, the sweetest girl in this world*
> *Is my Kookie-Nannie,*
> *Kookie-Nannie, Kook-Kook.*

Joy cooed and Daddy put his cap on her head and she pulled it off and laughed.

"Dinner break is over," came the call. "Back to the ropes! This schooner must be in the water before dark."

Refreshed, men took their places on the ropes and Mr. Brady played his fiddle.

Daddy and Mr. Harley put the little girls back on their blankets, where they enjoyed their evening naps.

"Pull, men, we're almost there. Pull. Pull."

Jackie ran closer to the shore, where a crowd gathered to watch the magnificent vessel about to enter the water. The First Lady stood at the water's edge, poised with a gold bag in her hand. Little children wearing colourful flowers in their hair jumped with excitement.

"Closer, closer," came the call, "and there she goes!"

Just as the schooner entered the water, the First Lady raised her hand with the gold bag and brought it down on the boat with a crashing sound.

People clapped and cheered and blew bugles and lit firecrackers.

"It's been christened!" Captain Bodden shouted. "The boat has been launched. She's in the water now, and I want to thank every person here for helping to make this a wonderful day."

Eventually the crowd began to dwindle, the cars creeping away. The Commissioner's car eased onto the marl road. Mr. Smiley walked away, his dusty feet clad in sandals made from old car tires and thatch straps. Beside him, Mr. Tindle moved along, his machete swinging in his hand, clearing the bush from the side of the road as he walked the long pathway to home. Each had a smile on his face. It was a day for everyone to remember.

Jackie glanced back toward the water, and in the rays of the Cayman sunset, the splendid schooner cast its first shadow on the sea.

GLOSSARY

BAMMY - of bread-like consistency made from grated cassava or yucca root, sprinkled with salt, squeezed dry and baked.

BREADFRUIT - a large, round, usually seedless fruit with a starchy pulp. When cooked it tastes similar to an Irish potato.

BREADFRUIT POD - brown and of a rough texture. Not edible.

BROOMWEED - cut from the rosemary bush, these flexible leafy stems were tied to broomsticks with thatch string and used to sweep sandyards.

CABOOSE - a wooden box built with four wooden legs and half filled with sand. Iron rods are stretched across the box to hold pots in place for cooking over burning sticks.

CALABASH - hollowed out gourd.

CASSAVA - also known as yucca.

COCONUT CREAM - the soft gel inside mature, but green coconuts.

COW-ITCH - brown fuzzy pods that grow wild, the fuzz blown by the wind. If it touches the skin, it causes severe itching.

CURLY BEANS - grow on vines inside pods resembling bean pods. Bright red and very hard tiny beans. Not edible.

DUPPY - Island slang for ghost.

FEVER GRASS - belonging to the lemon grass family. Makes excellent tea.

GRASS PIECE - a pasture

NAPPIES - baby diapers.

OBEAH - a form of witchcraft or magic.

PEAR - also known as avocado. Islanders know it as pear.

POPNUT TREE - large tree that grows beside the sea. Flowers are yellow and bell-shaped.

ROLLING CALF - fictitious monster used to scare small children, supposedly with chains attached to make noise as the fake monster traveled around.

SEA EGGS - or sea urchins with long stiff bristles that penetrate the feet when stepped on. They cling to rocks in the sea.

SEA GRAPE LEAF - a tough bright green leaf approximately eight inches around. Often used to roll in a cone shape and fill with sea grapes.

SEA GRAPE TREE - these grow to be very large trees and are usually found close to the sea.

SEA GRAPES - hang in bunches of about fifteen or twenty and fall from the tree when purple and ripe. Of the berry family.

SEA PIE - made from flour salt and water, the dough is kneaded, covered and set aside for about an hour. Small pieces are then cut and stretched to make homemade noodles.

SOLDIERS - or hermit type crabs that travel in straight lines like soldiers.

SWEETSOP - a round, green, bumpy fruit on the outside. When ripe it softens and the flesh is white and sweet on the inside.

UNNY - you all.